Untying the Knot

Also by Deborah Brodie

Writing Changes Everything: The 627 Best Things
Anyone Ever Said About Writing

Untying the Knot

Ex-Husbands, Ex-Wives

and Other Experts on the

Passage of Divorce

Edited by

Deborah Brodie

St. Martin's Griffin ☙ New York

Grateful acknowledgment is made for permission to reprint:

"Marriage Couplet" by William Cole, copyright © William Cole, 1956. Used by permission of the author.

Excerpt from "Divorce" by David Curzon, copyright © David Curzon, 1997. Used by permission of the author.

Excerpt from "Who She Was" by David Lehman, in *Valentine Place,* Scribner Paperback Poetry, copyright © David Lehman, 1996. Used by permission of the author.

"Separation & Divorce, ii" by Louis Phillips, copyright © Louis Phillips, 1967. Used by permission of the author.

Library of Congress Cataloging-in-Publication Data

Untying the knot : ex-husbands, ex-wives, and other experts on the
     passage of divorce / edited by Deborah Brodie.
                    p.   cm.
          ISBN 0-312-20042-0
          1. Marriage—Quotations, maxims, etc.   2. Divorce—Quotations,
     maxims, etc.   3. Marriage—Humor.   4. Divorce—Humor.
I. Brodie, Deborah.
     PN6084.M3U68   1999
     306.89—dc21   98-48160
                                                                        CIP

First St. Martin's Griffin Edition: February 1999

10   9   8   7   6   5   4   3   2   1

To Rachel, Hayim Daniel,

and Adam

Contents

Foreword

Getting through a divorce calls for the perfect companion: witty, compassionate, wise, endlessly tolerant of both storms and silence. No such human exists, but fortunately, *Untying the Knot* now does.

Who could ask for better company? Here are Zsa Zsa and Plutarch, the Bible and the Talmud, Heloise and Lenny Bruce ("Even if he finds you making out on the couch, *say it's your hairdresser*"). Plus poets and producers, lawyers and comedians, rabbis and therapists, sailors and social workers, whose disparate vantage points cover every stage of the divorce process, from the humiliating to the exhilarating.

Their words are welcome, because divorce is an enormous event, requiring nothing less than the reconfiguration of public and private identity. Its losses can evade description, just as language in which to celebrate its gains is often lacking. Depending on who's talking and when, divorce is a problem, a solution, a symptom, a salvation. It is a social issue so complex that advice columnist Ann Landers, informing her readers of her own impending divorce, wrote, "The lady with all the answers does not know the answers to this one."

There are, however, plenty of answers in this book, not least (at last) to the thorny question of how to respond to the declaration that, "I'm getting divorced." (Judith Martin, aka

Miss Manners, has abandoned "Oh, I am so sorry" for a more politic, "I wish you the best.") Or my own response (page 4) to that archly pitying question, "Don't you feel like you've failed?" Perhaps anthropologist Margaret Mead has the best answer: "I didn't have any failed marriages. I've been married three times and each marriage was successful."

The question hurts because, in the words of psychiatrist Frank Pittman, "It is not really possible to have change without crisis," and crises are no fun. As fellow shrink Peter Kramer puts it matter-of-factly, "The problem is not your choice, the problem is how you live with that choice. So the answer, stay or leave, turns on whether you think you can change."

Untying the Knot is for those who aspire to do so, and for the family and friends who support them, however painful the process or convoluted the path. Better than any imaginable guidebook is this distillation of human wisdom about separation and moving on. The milestones are all here: rueful acknowledgment of the persistence of love; stomach-churning grief at the ghostly marks where treasures once stood; delight at discovering the difference between loneliness and solitude. Present, too, are healing suggestions: why not a ritual for leaving a home, or one to bless its successor?

Some quotes are snack food, satisfying in small servings. Others offer entrée-size food for thought, like family therapist Stephen Lerner's potent analogy for assessing the effects of divorce on children: "People are left with the impression that they've initiated nuclear war on the family and now they're waiting to see what the extent of the radiation sickness will be." There's nothing like a divorce to bring out the cynic in us, the classic remark being Samuel Johnson's description of remarriage as "the triumph of hope over experience."

Jaded is easy, but *Untying the Knot* also documents the courage and conviction that shape new lives. There's romance (Katherine Hepburn: "Love has nothing to do with what you are expecting to get—only with what you're expecting to give—which is everything.") and realism (Rita Rudner: "Whenever I date a guy, I think, is this the man I want my children to spend their weekends with?"). And who could fault Lillian Vernon for wanting a wife?

Countering the myth that divorced people do not honor marriage, feminist Betty Friedan observes, "What people are seeking in marriage are among the best things we need and want." Whether met within marriage or without, these desires makes us human, and they are wonderfully set forth in the pages that follow.

—ASHTON APPLEWHITE, author of
*Cutting Loose: Why Women Who End
Their Marriages Do So Well*

Preface

Everyone knows someone—even more than one person—to give this book to. Half of all first marriages in the United States end in divorce, as do 60 percent of all second marriages, leaving thousands of family members, friends, therapists, and attorneys to provide comfort, commiseration, consolation.

When my editor, Marian Lizzi, came up with the idea for a book of quotes on divorce, in great excitement I immediately began to jot down a possible table of contents. My friends and grown children were all very encouraging. They viewed a new writing project as yet one more aspect of my full, rich life—my post-divorce life.

But it wasn't always like this. . . . When I was going through my divorce ten years ago, how I would have welcomed a book like this! Not a weighty treatise, but a collection of sound bites to show that a divorcing person is not alone, that she or he will live through it, and even laugh a bit.

During what English teacher Victoria Register calls "the marital meltdown," few people have energy for reading a long book. A collection of quotes, though, you can browse through or dip into as the mood allows. Open this book at any place, see what quotes you respond to, and know where you or your friends are, in both high and low moments.

For as much as divorce is about pain and stagnation, confusion and vulnerability, it is also about the process of getting through to the other side, about the immense possibilities for revisiting the old self who had a measure of sparkle, and about creating a new script for the next decade.

Not everyone quoted here is divorced. Not every quote was originally intended to reflect aspects of divorce. Some comments, however, were created specifically for this book, sometimes under a pseudonym, as people illuminated their own experiences and agreed to share them.

The almost 600 quotes come from personal experience and the experience of friends and acquaintances, self-help books, legal tomes, the Bible, novels, newspaper and magazine articles, scholarly studies, and celebrity biographies. The voices are not all in harmony; they contrast and disagree, just as a person in the midst of divorce can cry and laugh, rejoice and rant, all at the same time.

One friend asked if I got depressed while working on this book. The material did make me relive some of the sadness and even some of the anger, but depressed? No, because I knew that I was working toward that last chapter—on rebirth and renewal.

I am grateful for:

The generosity of my editor, Marian Lizzi, whose idea this was, and whose work, from the subtitle to the ending, reminds me of all that an editor can be.

The friends whose enthusiasm and insights helped shape and reshape this book: my vigorous agent, Carla M. Glasser; my rigorous colleagues, Judy Carey and Janet Pascal.

The friends who provided sources and suggestions: Francesca Belanger; Lisa Bernstein; David Curzon; Arlene and Howard Eisenberg; Carolyn Greene; Sharon Hancock; Elizabeth Law; David Lehman; Alexandra May; Kathleen Moses; Suzanne Newton; Virginia Norey; Louis Phillips; Diane Roback; Constance B. Sayre; Marilyn and Ray Weisberg, who gave me a clean well-lighted place to work.

The dedicated staff of St. Martin's Press: special events coordinator Harriet Seltzer, publicist Chris Ahearn, editorial assistant Alan S. Carl, art director and illustrator Michael Storrings.

The friends who saw me through my own divorce—we laughed, we cried, we redecorated: Laura Besserman; Ann A. Flowers; Vera and Morton Leifman; my community in Minyan M'at; Ann Schweninger; Mary E. Sunden; Burton L. Visotzky; my friend since kindergarten, Vicki L. Wayman; the late Marilyn Hirsh, may her memory be for a blessing, who knew my decision before I did.

The continuing support of my therapist, Helen Crohn; my attorney, Kenneth David Burrows; my parents, Edith and David Shapiro.

My friends and trusted advisors on both life and books— Sandee Brawarsky, Regina Hayes, Judith Herschlag Muffs, and Dina Rosenfeld—for savvy responses to the small details and the big picture.

My aunt Miriam and uncle Moshe Benjamin, and my cousins Michelle, Paul, Jeremy, Rebecca, and Adena Ruchames.

My children—Rachel Brodie, Hayim Daniel Brodie, and Adam Weisberg—their editorial suggestions, listening, talking, and gentle teasing are only part of the great blessing and delight of their sustaining love. This definitely doesn't say it all!

May we all share much joy in the future.

Untying the Knot

"Danger and Opportunity"

Some Definitions of Divorce

The Chinese define stress as the balance between danger and opportunity. In our country, that's the definition of divorce.

—ABIGAIL TRAFFORD, *journalist*

Divorce: Fission after fusion.

—RITA MAE BROWN, *novelist*

Divorce is a process, not a single event.

—VICKI LANSKY, *nonfiction writer*

Divorce is not the sinking of the ship. It's more like the oil spill that follows, and the cleanup goes on indefinitely.

—WALTER L. KANTROWITZ, *attorney,*
and HOWARD EISENBERG, *writer*

Divorce is like gridlock. It takes forever to get through.

—Erzsi Deak, *writer*

Nowadays love is a matter of chance, matrimony a matter of money, and divorce a matter of course.

—Helen Rowland, *journalist,* in *Reflections of a Bachelor Girl,* 1903

Marriage no longer is considered to be so permanent—"till death do us part" has been replaced with "till death of the marriage parts us."

—Florence W. Kaslow, *therapist*

The virtually universal understanding is that the breakdown of a marriage is irretrievable if one spouse says it is.

—Mary Ann Glendon, *legal scholar*

What does the promise of a permanent commitment mean when everyone knows it's provisional? I am tempted to say that divorce makes marriage meaningless—which doesn't mean I would wish there to be less divorce, just less marriage.

—Phyllis Rose, *professor of English*

Divorce is about the apportionment of two "things" (for lack of a better word): money and kids.

—Michael Leshin, *family law attorney*

Divorce is a game played by lawyers.

—CARY GRANT, *actor,* divorced four times

It is always a soap opera. No matter who you are or what has gone into your life, the end of a marriage becomes, when meted out in words, the same old story.

—MARY CANTWELL, *journalist*

Divorces are made in Heaven.

—OSCAR WILDE, *dramatist,* in *The Importance of Being Earnest*

For a while we pondered whether to take a vacation or to get a divorce. We decided that a trip to Bermuda is over in two weeks, but a divorce is something you always have.

—WOODY ALLEN, *filmmaker and humorist,* divorced twice

I was given the secret handshake to the world's largest club. The Divorced. We were everywhere.

—ANN PATCHETT, *novelist*

It is always tough to end a relationship. It's like moving away from an apartment that you have just built up. Are you being evicted or are you looking for a place with better standards? Either way, it's a hell of a thing.

—DOUG E. FRESH, *hip-hop pioneer*

Modern divorce is little more than a functional substitute for death. . . . In the seventeenth century the remarriage rate, made possible by death, was not far off that in our own day, made possible by divorce.

—LAWRENCE STONE, *social historian*

Divorce evokes more anger than death, and it is, of course, considerably more optional.

—JUDITH VIORST, *writer*

The death of a marriage is like the death of a person: Who my friends were when they were together, their joined spirit, is gone.

—SY SAFRANSKY, *journalist*

The end of a marriage is a loss, but not a failure. On the contrary it is a victory—over inertia, terror, conformity, insecurity, and countless other demons.

—ASHTON APPLEWHITE, *writer*

Being divorced is like being hit by a Mack truck—if you survive you start looking very carefully to the right and left.

—JEAN KERR, *playwright,* in *Mary, Mary*

"Impossible to Live With"

Why Divorce?

Everyone is nearly impossible to live with.

—SHARYN WOLF, *couples counselor*

In Biblical times, a man could have as many wives as he could afford. Just like today.

—ABIGAIL VAN BUREN, *Dear Abby*

The modern age runs much on the instalment plan, and we are applying the same plan to matrimony. . . . If present tendencies continue much further a divorce coupon for the convenience of the couple will be attached to each marriage license.

—ROBERT GRANT, in *Good Housekeeping,* September 1921

In the old days, no one got divorced. We worked it out. We believed in the sanctity of a mistake!

—*Borscht Belt joke*

We are in the act of trying out—and failing miserably at it—one of the most pathological experiments that a civilized society has ever imagined, namely, the basing of marriage which is lasting upon romance which is a passing fancy.

—DENIS DE ROUGEMENT, *French scholar*

The clearest explanation for the failure of any marriage is that the two people are incompatible; that is, one is male and the other female.

—ANNA QUINDLEN, *journalist and novelist*

Men are from Mars, women are from Venus.

—JOHN GRAY, *relationship expert*

With the education and elevation of women we shall have a mighty sundering of the unholy ties that hold men and women together who loathe and despise each other.

—ELIZABETH CADY STANTON, *women's rights leader,* 1868

If divorce has increased by one thousand percent, don't blame the women's movement. Blame the obsolete sex roles on which our marriages were based.

—BETTY FRIEDAN, *feminist and writer*

Divorce is less common where women and men are economically dependent on one another—most notably in societies that use the plow for agriculture. In such societies, spouses need each other to make ends meet.

—HELEN E. FISHER, *anthropologist*

Couples who are open to living together are often more open to divorce [after they marry] because they've practiced being in a relationship without permanent commitment.

—GEORGIA WITKIN, *therapist*

We are the only animal species that cannot seem to figure out how to pair off and raise children without maiming ourselves in the process.

—ANNE ROIPHE, *novelist*

We believe lesbian and gay couples deserve the option to marry. Many already behave like married couples, but legalizing same-sex marriage would change the world around them, and, we believe, make divorce less likely.

—STEVIE BRYANT and DEMIAN, *publishers*

Where they love they do not desire and where they desire they cannot love.

—SIGMUND FREUD, *psychoanalyst*

One of the arguments for the high divorce rate of our time is that people now live so long—or as one wag put it, "Every marriage ends in divorce—it is just that some people die before they have that opportunity."

—DAVID POPENOE, *professor of sociology*

One man who came to me for advice because he was contemplating a divorce told me mournfully why he thought the marriage went wrong. He said, "I know what my problem was. I was looking for a Ferrari and I got a Ford." I said, "I think the problem was you were looking for a car."

—DAVID AARON, *rabbi*

The trouble with some women is that they get all excited about nothing—and then marry him.

—CHER, *actor and singer*

Although they say that opposites attract, I have never read that they should marry.

—ANN HOOD, *novelist*

I was impatient. I wanted instant gratification, and I didn't want to wait for it, either.

—LAWRENCE BLOCK, *mystery writer*

Being on the other side of a relationship with someone like me must be difficult.

—DONALD TRUMP, *real estate mogul,* on divorcing his second wife, Marla Maples

Nothing she could do would change him. Take him, leave him, or take him and hold it against him. These were her choices.

—JUDITH SILLS, *clinical psychologist*

Love often fails because people instinctively give what they want.

—JOHN GRAY, *relationship expert*

A complete sharing between two people is an impossibility and whenever it seems, nevertheless, to exist, it is a narrowing, a mutual agreement which robs either one member or both of his fullest freedom and development.

—RAINER MARIA RILKE, *poet*

When two people grow apart in love, it's usually only one who is growing.

—SHARON WEGSCHEIDER-CRUSE, *therapist*

You did the best you could with what you had to work with in your relationship. You could only say you'd failed if you'd planted a seed in fertile soil. But if you dropped that seed on a rock, it's the rock, not you, that prevented the seed from growing.

—MIRA KIRSHENBAUM, *psychotherapist*

Divorce after sixty is likely to mean one or both partners feel imprisoned—not enough space between them to breathe, too much togetherness, and no separate hobbies, trips, or learning experiences; too *much* acceptance of limitations.

—EDA LESHAN, *family counselor and writer*

At first his jealousy was a compliment, then it became a prison.

—MARY D. LANKFORD, *librarian*

I married a man who left me feeling lonely not because he wasn't home but because he *was*.

—DAPHNE MERKIN, *essayist*

The fear of making permanent commitments can change the mutual love of husband and wife into two loves of self, two loves existing side by side until they end in separation.

—Pope John Paul II

Fifty percent or more of marriages go bust because most of us no longer have extended families. When you marry somebody now, all you get is one person. I say that when couples fight, it isn't about sex or power. What they're really saying is, "You're not enough people!"

—Kurt Vonnegut, *novelist,* in *Timequake*

He who therefore seeks to part, is one who highly honors the married life and would not stain it: and the reasons which now move him to divorce are equal to the best of those that could first warrant him to marry.

—John Milton, *poet and essayist,* in *The Doctrine and Discipline of Divorce*

We were a perfect couple; I was always feeling guilty and he blamed me for everything.

—Penny Kaganoff, *editor and journalist*

Nothing is too small to have a power struggle over.

—Sharyn Wolf, *couples counselor*

When things were getting pretty bad in my second marriage, my wife said, "You know, Ira, what you *really* want is a 'Stepford Wife.'" I got shot down with my own book title!

—IRA LEVIN, *novelist*

I became successful so suddenly I got much more macho. I suddenly felt like a strong man. That altered everything between us.

—NORMAN MAILER, *novelist,* on his marriage to the first of six wives

Our lives were always bursting apart and dispersing. Acting couples generally don't stay together because of this element of separation. I remember once coming home after a four-month tour and Jeanne leaving the next day for a play in Scandinavia.

—JEAN-LOUIS RICHARD, *actor,* on his marriage to actor Jeanne Moreau

The partner of a performing artist can't have too many personal needs—it messes up the idea that *you're* the important one.

—KATE JOHNSON, *opera singer*

Music is my mistress and she plays second fiddle to no one.

—DUKE ELLINGTON, *jazz musician,* divorced twice

[I made] the mistake of thinking that each of my wives was my mother, that there would never be a replacement once she left.

—CARY GRANT, *actor,* divorced four times

I still love you. I'll always love you. But it isn't ring-a-ding-ding anymore. Do you understand?

—ELIZABETH TAYLOR, *actor,* to MICHAEL WILDING, the second of eight husbands

Partially it was youth, and partially it was adulthood.

—ISABELLA ROSSELLINI, *actor and model,* on the failure of her marriage to director Martin Scorsese

There's no doubt in my mind that the essential problems between Grant [Tinker] and me were aggravated by alcohol-provoked arguments. They were never resolved as neither of us could remember them the next morning. The death knell of our seventeen-year marriage was sounded by ice cubes.

—MARY TYLER MOORE, *actor*

I kissed and kissed and kissed but after thirteen years he was still a frog.

—"Alice," in *Creative Divorce* by MEL KRANTZLER

Passion, Morning Breath, and Broken Plates

Expectations of Love and Marriage

We all have this idealized version of love, but the reality is fighting, passion, bad breath in the morning, and breaking plates.

—Boy George, *musician*

Love does not conquer all. It doesn't even conquer most.

—Judith Sills, *clinical psychologist*

As with most couples, they are like two people jumping out of an airplane clasped together, each believing the other to be a parachute.

—Alison Lurie, *novelist,* in *Love and Friendship*

Let's take the cup of hemlock now.

—ERNEST HEMINGWAY, *novelist,* at his wedding to his fourth wife

If you want to read about love and marriage, you've got to buy two separate books.

—ALAN KING, *comedian*

People should be required to reenact marriage every five years or so, like signing a lease.

—MARILYN FRENCH, *novelist,* in *The Women's Room*

I see us married for one day at a time.

—BRUCE WILLIS, *actor,* a few months before separating from his wife of ten years, actor Demi Moore

Marriage at its lowest: We regard it as a sort of friendship recognized by the police.

—ROBERT LOUIS STEVENSON, *novelist and poet*

Getting married is just the first step toward getting divorced.

—ZSA ZSA GABOR, *actor,* divorced eight times

Marriage is a divorce waiting to happen.

—JEANNE DE SAINTE MARIE, *writer*

We acted as if marriage was the end of having to work on our relationship, when it was just the beginning.

—EVELYN McDONNELL, *writer*

Women hope men will change after marriage but they don't; men hope women won't change but they do.

—BETTINA ARNDT, *journalist*

You never have a better marriage than your parents'.

—RICHARD PECK, *novelist*

There is always something to talk about when one is falling in love. And so often there is not in the long-haul mechanics of marriage.

—TIM PARKS, *nonfiction writer*

Phyllis: We won't wait long.
Strephon: No. We might change our minds. We'll get married first.
Phyllis: And change our minds afterwards?
Strephon: That's the usual course.

—W. S. GILBERT, *dramatist,* in *Iolanthe*

Before you get married, know whom you will divorce.

—*Yiddish proverb*

Both marriage and death ought to be welcome: the one promises happiness, doubtless the other assures it.

—MARK TWAIN, *humorist*

Marriage presents one of the most difficult personal problems in human life; the most emotional as well as the most romantic of all human dreams has to be consolidated into an ordinary working relationship.

—BRONISLAW MALINOWSKI, *anthropologist*

We both struggled with the romantic ideal. We used to coo at each other through clenched teeth.

—BENJAMIN H. CHEEVER, *novelist and journalist*

We had all those romantic ideas about marriage, just like heterosexuals, but got into lots of trouble with the butch-fem kind of stuff. Since I had been married I just assumed Ted would do what my wife had. What a mistake that was!

—"Anonymous," in *The Male Couple* by DAVID P. MCWHIRTER and ANDREW M. MATTISON, *therapists*

Why do people expect to be happily married when they are not individually happy? How do you expect mankind to be happy in pairs when it is so miserable separately?

—PETER DE VRIES, *novelist*, in *Reuben, Reuben*

Love has nothing to do with what you are expecting to get—only with what you are expecting to give—which is everything.

—Katharine Hepburn, *actor*

Who are happy in marriage? Those with so little imagination that they cannot picture a better state, and those so shrewd that they prefer quiet slavery to hopeless rebellion.

—H. L. Mencken, *writer and critic*

Marriage has been for forever for, well, *forever.* It hasn't adapted, hasn't moved with the times. Heck, cars used to last 20 years. You see any carmakers offering 20-year warranties these days?

—Michael Beninger, *writer*

The shattering of a glass under the *huppah* [marriage canopy] injects a note of sorrow into one of life's happiest events. Today the breaking of the glass [is] also symbolic of the potential for breakup of the new marriage.

—Rivka Haut, *women's advocate*

Everyone's first marriage [is] a fiasco.

—Olivia Goldsmith, *novelist,* in *The Bestseller*

Sometimes I wonder if men and women really suit each other. Perhaps they should live next door and just visit now and then.

—KATHARINE HEPBURN, *actor*

We're not kids; we know what forever means. (Oh, god, it means we *never get to sleep with anyone else again!*)

—MARJORIE INGALL, *writer*

Love is eternal as long as it lasts.

—VINICIUS DE MORALIS, *songwriter*

Marriage feels like the ultimate delusion, a precooked TV dinner with compartments full of impossibilities like "forever" and "completeness" and "ultimate fulfillment."

—REBECCA LEVENTHAL WALKER, *writer*

When people ask me how we've lived past one hundred, I say, "Honey, we never married. We never had husbands to worry us to death."

—BESSIE DELANEY, age 101, referring to herself
and her sister, Sadie, age 103

The test of a good marriage is not compatibility in bed, but compatibility in life.

—MAURICE LAMM, *rabbi*

The most seductive sentence in the English language isn't "I love you" but "I understand you."

—J. D. McClatchy, *poet*

As the husband is, the wife is: thou art mated with a
   clown,
And the grossness of his nature will have weight to
   drag thee down.
He will hold thee, when his passion shall have spent
   its novel force,
Something better than his dog, a little dearer than
   his horse.

—Alfred Tennyson, *poet,* in "Locksley Hall"

Any intelligent woman who reads the marriage contract, and then goes into it, deserves all the consequences.

—Isadora Duncan, *dancer*

The origin of the wedding ring represents part of a chain binding the wife to her master. Beware. Stop, look, listen and be cautious.

—Margarita Prentice, *Washington state senator*

In Hollywood a marriage is a success if it outlasts milk.

—Rita Rudner, *comedian*

I can't run down marriage. My weakness was in staying with mine as long as I did. But what people are seeking in marriage are among the best things we need and want.

—Betty Friedan, *feminist and writer*

The silken texture of the marriage tie bears a daily strain of wrong and insult to which no other human relation can be subjected without lesion.

—William Dean Howells, *writer and editor*

He's the kind of man a woman would have to marry to get rid of.

—Mae West, *actor*

Conventional modern marriage—an eternal commitment with loopholes galore—expresses precisely the degree of loss of autonomy that we are able to tolerate.

—Peter D. Kramer, *psychiatrist*

To be happy in a relationship which imposes so many impediments on her, as traditional marriage does, a woman must be slightly mentally ill.

—Jessie Bernard, *sociologist*

What about treating a marriage somewhat like a mortgage? In order to succeed, you'd only have to make it to the first renegotiation point. If it doesn't work out, you cut a new deal.

—Michael Beninger, *writer*

No matter who you marry, you wake up married to someone else.

—DAMON RUNYON, *playwright,* in *Guys and Dolls*

There is no housework on the honeymoon. No housework is the definition of the honeymoon!

—SHARYN WOLF, *couples counselor*

The camel's straw was probably the afternoon I reminded [my husband] of our prebaby agreement—fifty-fifty with the child care. His surprising reply was: "Fifty percent of the time means you take care of Jesse until he's ten years old, and then I take the next ten years."

—TWYLA THARP, *choreographer*

Husbands are like fires. They go out when unattended.

—ZSA ZSA GABOR, *actor,* divorced eight times

The question of housework is not a trivial matter to be worked out the day before we go on to greater things. Men do not want equality at home. A strong woman is a threat, an inconvenience, and she can be replaced.

—JANE O'REILLY, *justice of the peace*

Most women work one shift at the office or factory and a "second shift" at home.

—ARLIE HOCHSCHILD, *sociologist*

Housework represents for men merely a negative and inconsequential moment from which they quickly escape.

—SIMONE DE BEAUVOIR, *writer and feminist*

Any man today who returns from work, sinks into a chair, and calls for his pipe is a man with an appetite for danger.

—BILL COSBY, *comedian*

For each of the daily household tasks which the husband performs at least half the time, the wife is about 3 percent less likely to have thoughts of divorce.

—JOAN HUBER and GLENNA SPITZE, *social researchers*

When demand begins, love departs.

—ELIYAHU DESSLER, *rabbi*

They proved to be part of a mismatched team. When one horse is pulling both along, no good can come of it. I have also noticed that the woman usually pulls more than her share.

—RITA MAE BROWN, *novelist,* in *Dolley*

A house unkept cannot be so distressing as a life unlived.

—ROSE MACAULAY, *writer*

The graveyards are full of women whose houses were so spotless you could eat off the floor. Remember the second wife always has a maid.

—HELOISE CRUSE, *housekeeping columnist*

I have too many fantasies to be a housewife.

—MARILYN MONROE, *actor,* on her marriage to baseball player Joe DiMaggio

Marriage is the best magician there is. In front of your eyes, it can change an exciting, cute little dish into a boring dishwasher.

—RYAN O'NEAL, *actor*

I have yet to hear a man ask for advice on how to combine marriage and a career.

—GLORIA STEINEM, *journalist and feminist*

"I hate discussions of feminism that end up with who does the dishes," she said. So do I. But at the end, there are always the damned dishes.

—MARILYN FRENCH, *novelist,* in *The Women's Room*

"The Unseen Rival"

Affairs

In any triangle, who is the betrayer, who the unseen rival, and who the humiliated lover? Oneself, oneself, and no one but oneself!

—ERICA JONG, *novelist,* in *How to Save Your Own Life*

What can I do? I'm hot.

—JACK NICHOLSON, *actor,* confronted by actor Anjelica Huston over his affairs with younger women

What attracts me is not women, the simple desire for other women, it is the idea of options, the desire for unlimited choices. To choose to remain with one woman is to accept the limited world of old age.

—STEPHEN DOBYNS, *novelist*

Hogamous higamous
Men are polygamous
Higamous hogamous
Women monogamous.

—Ann Pinchot, *writer*

That long-term monogamy is unnatural is something every male of the species has felt. Yet where would we be without some repression?

—TIM PARKS, *nonfiction writer*

A lie by day, a lie by night, a lie in every touch and every look; a lie in every caress and every quarrel; a lie in every word and in every silence.

—EDITH WHARTON, *novelist,* in *The Age of Innocence*

When a man cheats, we assume it's all about a new naked body, but when a woman does it, we assume it's for love.

—KATIE ROIPHE, *writer*

Women are more likely to use the word love to justify adultery to themselves. You have to be in love. Otherwise you're a whore.

—ELEANOR ALTER, *divorce lawyer*

Adultery is a delightful way to spend the afternoon. It's sociable and nonfattening.

> —GAEL GREENE, *restaurant critic*

Women are motivated by the same forces as men—loneliness, hostility, boredom, the need to feel younger and attractive, the need to be worshipped.

> —RAOUL LIONEL FELDER, *divorce lawyer*

Even if he finds you making out on the couch, *say it's your hairdresser.*

> —LENNY BRUCE, *comedian*

It is true that nothing substitutes for the divine insanity of a new sexual love. It is also true that, under certain circumstances, a new sexual love can make you sickeningly anxious, destroy your family, infect you with disease, cost you a fortune, isolate your socially, or just plain break your heart. With that in mind, there's a lot to be said for the thrill of rock climbing.

> —JUDITH SILLS, *clinical psychologist*

No man can really be sure of any wife. If this is so, it is the end of the world.

> —ISAAC BASHEVIS SINGER, *short story writer,* in "The Recluse"

Come, let us take our fill of love until the morning; let us delight in amorous embrace. For my husband is not at home; he is off on a long journey.

—*The "alien woman" of Proverbs 7:18–19*

Just two people, that's all, and we ended adultery in Kandahar [Afghanistan] forever. Even 100,000 police could not have the effect that we achieved with one punishment of this kind.

—ALHAJ MAULAVI QALAMUDDIN, *head of the religious police,* on the stoning of two people accused of adultery, 1997

If your husband shuts off the computer every time you walk into the room, it definitely sounds like he's hiding something. Confront him with your suspicions. I guarantee you'll be able to tell by his reaction what the truth is.

—IVANA TRUMP, *socialite and advice columnist,* to a woman who suspected her husband was cheating on-line.

An affair *always* means something, and it often means you are in an angry marriage.

—BONNIE MASLIN, *psychotherapist*

I saw what he'd done as abuse, and even attended a meeting of the "codependent spouses of alcoholics," since there were no groups for the codependent spouses of cheaters.

—SUSAN SPANO, *travel writer*

I'm a mass of contradictions. I change my mind all the time. So tell [whatever] man I'm looking for that if he likes to have affairs with lots of women, then I'm perfect for him.

—Barbra Streisand, *singer and director,* before meeting and marrying actor James Brolin

If someone is very special to you, is it really that important if every now and then he takes off and has a liaison with someone else? I mean, is it really catastrophic?

—Susan Sarandon, *actor*

It's a thing about being men; we both had to see what was good for the gander is good for the other gander, too. We learned there was no goose, just we two ganders.

—"Joe," in *The Male Couple,* by David P. McWhirter and Andrew M. Mattison, *therapists*

Fidelity is possible. Anything is possible if you're stubborn and strong. But it's not that important. Traditional marriage is very outdated. I don't think people should live together the rest of their lives suppressing frustrations.

—Michelle Pfeiffer, *actor*

When you work in a candy store, your appetite for candy tends to diminish after a while.

—Bob Guccione, *Penthouse magazine publisher*

Thank you for letting me live again.

> —PRINCESS MARGARET to her lover, Robin Douglas-Home

If you yourself are playing around, then your conscience is eased if your partner does the same.

> —JOCELYN STEVENS, *friend of Anthony Armstrong-Jones,*
> *Lord Snowden,* on his encouraging his wife,
> Princess Margaret, to have an affair

[My first wife] accused me of cheating on her, which I had not. But once accused, I thought I might as well.

> —KELSEY GRAMMER, *actor*

You want monogamy, marry a swan.

> —NORA EPHRON, *novelist and screenwriter,* in *Heartburn*

The affair may enable us to need less from the man to whom we are married, and therefore to love him more.

> —JUDITH SILLS, *clinical psychologist*

There's nothing like a shameful secret to fire a man up.

> —SAUL BELLOW, *novelist*

My Pattern with Women: Need to step into danger. Something to bring me adrenaline—a rush. I lie—pretend—mislead—equivocate—I will have two or more women going at the same time. . . . I have secret compartmentalized little worlds I keep away from each other.

—LARRY KING, *talk-show host,* married seven times

Fidelity seems to be a trait in short supply with most men, male "equipment" being able to rise to stimulating opportunities with alacrity.

—JOAN COLLINS, *actor and novelist*

When [an interviewer] asked my wife about the young women in my life, she said that I travel all the time and I might look at another bowl of pasta or another pretty face, but, she added, "there is still plenty of linguine at home."

—LUCIANO PAVAROTTI, *opera singer,* two years before leaving his wife of 35 years for his 28-year-old assistant

When you base marriage solely on love, you raise the possibility that a new love can always tempt you out of marriage.

—ABIGAIL TRAFFORD, *journalist*

I found a letter. Like countless other wives, I found a letter. Without my reading glasses, I could see only the kisses at the end and thought it was one of mine. Then I saw Ed standing in the doorway. His face told me everything.

—Barbara Malley, *writer*

I don't go around breaking up marriages. Besides, you can't break up a happy marriage.

—Elizabeth Taylor, *actor,* before her marriage to singer Eddie Fisher

I don't sleep with married men, but what I mean is that I don't sleep with happily married men.

—Britt Ekland, *actor*

There will be scars. It is never the same after one person has strayed.

—Ivana Trump, *socialite and advice columnist*

I love Henry and I love you. I know I'm supposed to think it's wrong, but instead I think it's *mine.* It's my destiny, and my complication.

—Laurie Colwin, *novelist,* in *Family Happiness*

Sometimes you have to do the wrong thing just to know you're alive.

—Richard Ford, *novelist,* in *Wildlife*

I think it takes two people to hurt you: the one who does it and the one who tells you.

—Nora Ephron, *novelist,* in *Heartburn*

"The Sound of the Handcuffs Going Click"

Self-Esteem and Self-Erasure

The process of self-erasure in a relationship happens in small, almost imperceptible increments, one isolated incident after another. It's so subtle, and there's so much background noise that you don't even hear the sound of the handcuffs going click.

—DIANA HUME GEORGE, *English professor*

O wife, I must be myself. I cannot break my self any longer for you.

—RALPH WALDO EMERSON, *essayist*

If Jennifer had from the first insisted on being her true self, the marriage would have had much more strife and much more hope.

—CARL ROGERS, *psychologist*

Women have to know their own inner worth. The men want to marry them, and the women shouldn't look at themselves as furniture. The woman with a sense of her own value has a much better chance than the one who thinks of the marriage as her salvation.

—STANFORD LOTWIN, *divorce lawyer*

I had ambitions, but I kept them hidden. It was after all the early 1950s. Rosie the Riveter of World War II days had in most instances turned in her welding torch for a waffle iron.

—LILLIAN VERNON, *entrepreneur,* divorced twice

She's hot, and I'm lukewarm.

—SAUL BELLOW, *novelist,* about his fourth wife's greater skill in calculus

You can't go on and on for years being miserable about a situation and not have it change you. You get so you can't stand yourself.

—LUCILLE BALL, *comedian,* on her decision to divorce actor Desi Arnaz

When I was a wife, I didn't like who I was.

—ASHTON APPLEWHITE, *writer*

When a man makes a woman his wife, it is the greatest compliment he can give her. And usually the last.

—HELEN ROWLAND, *journalist*

[The prenuptial agreement] was about someone trying to control your life—even after he wasn't in it. Everybody was thinking that I'd get locked in a room with my white dress on and just sign it. Wrong. I put on a black dress and went downstairs to have lunch with my guests.

—DEBORAH HUGHES, *publicist,* about the wedding she called off

I'm not saying self-esteem requires us to put ourselves above our loved ones. But I am saying self-esteem means including ourselves on our list of loved ones.

—GEORGIA WITKIN, *therapist*

If I am not for myself, who is for me? But if I care only for myself, what am I?

—HILLEL, *first-century rabbi*

Sometimes it is less hard to wake up feeling lonely when you are alone than to wake up feeling lonely when you are with someone.

—LIV ULLMANN, *actor*

When men pull away from women, they don't know who they are. Or they identify with things that are completely bizarre, like football. And beer. You know?

—SAM SHEPARD, *playwright*

Mutuality is a worthy ideal. But if we do not reward it elsewhere—if in the school and office and marketplace, we celebrate self-assertion—it seems worrisome to ask the institution of marriage to play by different rules.

—PETER D. KRAMER, *psychiatrist*

If [a wife] lets herself go, if she gains two more pounds, if she does not keep her stocking seams straight, she will lose her husband. It is incredible that so many families have stayed together.

—MARGARET MEAD, *anthropologist*

If a man says something in the forest and his wife isn't there to hear it, is he still wrong?

—*Caller on "Car Talk," National Public Radio*

The loss of the most important relationship of my life was the price I paid for coming to know myself.

—CLAIRE BLOOM, *actor,* on her divorce from novelist Philip Roth

A frog, dropped in hot water, jumps out and saves itself; but a frog put in water that is heated *very gradually* stays there and boils to death.

—GLORIA STEINEM, *journalist and feminist*

Only two things my ex-wife didn't like about me: everything I said, and everything I did.

—John Briley, *sailor*

"All Things Are Possible"

Therapy

All things are possible, from reconciliation to termination. Nonetheless, counselors note that in most cases by the time a couple seeks counseling, it is too late.

—DIANE VAUGHAN, *sociologist*

It takes more than two to keep two together.

—ROBERT TAIBBI, *social worker*

Married couples, at the beginning of treatment, tend to use the counseling situation as an arena for an extension of their customary modes of conflict.

—GERALD APPEL, *psychotherapist*

I have a rule of thumb about guilt. It is useful if it doesn't last more than five minutes and produces some change in behavior.

—BOB BEAVERS, *family therapist*

Often a marital therapist may feel like a labor negotiator, or a diplomat involved in conflictual issues. He may find himself taking sides whether he likes it or not.

—JAY HALEY, *therapist*

We see so many people make the same mistakes in a second marriage that the attitude has become: hold on, work harder at the one you've got, unless it's utterly hopeless.

—HAROLD LIEF, *psychiatrist*

Divorce without first attempting a reconciliation with a marriage counselor isn't much smarter than amputating a leg because of a bunion.

—WALTER L. KANTROWITZ, *attorney,* and HOWARD EISENBERG, *writer*

It is not really possible to have change without crisis.

—FRANK PITTMAN, *psychiatrist*

While motivated to seek help from the therapist and perhaps experiencing positive feelings toward him, a husband may well see the therapist as a sexual competitor in a situation in which his masculinity is challenged.

—GERALD APPEL, *psychotherapist*

If they don't like each other's odor, no matter how much therapy I do with them, the chances of that relationship working are fairly low.

—SUSAN SCHIFFMAN, *professor of medical psychology*

In the age of the binuclear family, home is no longer the place you go to when nobody else will take you in. In many families, it can be pretty tricky just figuring out where home is. Sometimes it's easier to go to your therapist's office.

—RICHARD SIMON, *therapist and editor*

Much to my irritation, my therapist never coughed up any of the direct advice I blatantly fished for. Growth is painful, and the responsibility is the patient's, on the couch as in life.

—ASHTON APPLEWHITE, *writer*

Any effort to turn a particular family into someone's idea of the ideal, or even the norm, would be as cruel and crazy as the Procrustean bed. Procrusteus was the legendary innkeeper who had a bed of a certain size, and put each of his guests through the process of either carving them down or stretching them out to fit his bed. Therapists who attempt that are no more welcome than innkeepers who do so.

—FRANK PITTMAN, *psychiatrist*

While counselors can describe the general trends they observe among their clients, like sociologists, they are unable to predict what's going to happen in the individual case.

—DIANE VAUGHAN, *sociologist*

Couples are incompatible by nature. But it is this very incompatibility that brings up all of the possibilities of healing and growth.

—HARVILLE HENDRIX, *psychotherapist*

Analytic insights are like Chinese food. Two hours later, I'll feel hungry again.

—ERICA JONG, *novelist,* in *How to Save Your Own Life*

"Nuclear War on the Family"

Expectations of Divorce

People are left with the impression that they've initiated nuclear war on the family and now they're waiting to see what the extent of the radiation sickness will be.

—STEPHEN LERNER, *family therapist*

Americans idealize lifelong marriage; they equate divorce with failure.

—HELEN E. FISHER, *anthropologist*

At the wedding, they're selling themselves into bondage. With the divorce, you're giving them happiness, release, a chance to make a better life for themselves.

—RAOUL LIONEL FELDER, *divorce attorney*

There is no such thing as a perfect divorce, any more than there is a perfect marriage.

—MARY ROGERS, *financial counselor*

The divorced woman suggests, by her very presence, a threat to the status quo; she carries with her the lack of conviction about so important a decision as who she should marry. Worse yet, there is the dark aura of her singleness, and the accompanying spector of emotional neediness. Worst of all, she intimates at the possibility that the marriages around her are themselves as likely to fall apart as not.

—DAPHNE MERKIN, *essayist*

Being divorced and a nonsmoker is only slightly less dangerous than smoking a pack or more of cigarettes a day and staying married.

—DAVID LARSON, *health researcher*

There's no innocence in divorce. *Everyone* is a victim.

—RICHARD GILMAN, *drama professor*

Dear Seattle Friend: Interesting that going to jail creates 10 stress points less than getting a divorce—and only 13 more than getting married! I'll bet some convicts would disagree.

—ANN LANDERS, *advice columnist*

There is no such thing as a win or victory in settling your divorce. If you can both walk away feeling only somewhat dissatisfied, then it was probably a fair outcome.

—VICKI LANSKY, *nonfiction writer*

The divorce will be gayer than the wedding.

—COLETTE, *novelist,* in *Cheri*

"Misery Could Begin"

Making the Decision

I wake up every morning wondering if today one of us will make the move. Torture would be over and misery could begin.

—JULIA PHILLIPS, *movie producer*

When you reach a fork in the road, take it.

—YOGI BERRA, *baseball player*

I fantasize about how wonderful it would be to be a widow, pitied and coddled by a warm and loving community, rid of a mean husband without the disgrace and mess of a divorce. Not long after that I leave him.

—PENNY KAGANOFF, *editor and journalist*

I knew I could never get divorced. I couldn't stand the paperwork.

—MARY MORRIS, *travel writer*

I love you and I hate you. "Why?" you may ask.
I know not, I know only that it is so, and I am in
agony.

—CATULLUS, *Roman poet*

"Where're you going?" Desi wanted to know. "To court, to divorce you," I told him. "Lucy," he said, "the next time I marry, I'm going to be a better husband." "And the next time I marry, I'm going to be a better wife," I answered truthfully. Desi's face brightened. "Then why don't we both try it on each other?" he suggested.

—LUCILLE BALL, *comedian,* before a brief predivorce reconciliation

As our marriage unraveled, I considered having a baby as a way of holding on to the only life I knew. A baby or a divorce—it would be one or the other. It was the other, and after five years together we separated.

—SANDRA HURTES, *writer*

I am tonight the mystery guest
At a dinner thrown
By my own
Decisions.

—KELSEY GRAMMER, *actor*

Bad enough to choose once in a lifetime whom to live with; to go on choosing, to reaffirm one's choice day after day, as one must when it is culturally possible to divorce, is really asking a lot of people.

—PHYLLIS ROSE, *professor of English*

Any marriage worthy of the name entails repeated remarriage, active choices to stay on in the face of new perspectives on self and spouse.

—PETER D. KRAMER, *psychiatrist*

When the choice is to die or to divorce, it isn't always the clearest choice in the world.

—ANN PATCHETT, *novelist*

If it never was very good, it will never be very good—where are the good things going to come from that you have a right to look forward to? When it comes to relationships, you can fix what was broken, but you can rarely fix what never worked in the first place.

—MIRA KIRSHENBAUM, *psychotherapist*

Even though the tree tries to stay steady, there are winds blowing all around it.

—*Vietnamese proverb*

When a spouse—particularly the wife—rolls her eyes while the other is talking, the marital EXIT sign is blinking fiercely.

—Francine Russo, *writer*

We are separating not to destroy our marriage but to save it.

—Barbra Streisand, *singer and director,* before a predivorce reconciliation with actor Elliott Gould

If you realize that marriage is impossible, and you've gone through counseling and a trial separation, then unload the bum.

—Ann Landers, *advice columnist*

I had wanted to leave my marriage for years, had saved it up like a sweet before bedtime, like a piece of bubble gum put on the childhood bedpost.

—Erica Jong, *novelist,* in *How to Save Your Own Life*

My sister and I had a litmus test: when the key turns in the door—don't give yourself a moment to think—what is your gut response? Are you happy he's home? Or are you miserable?

—Dvorah Telushkin, *memoirist*

I knew I would never be given my freedom. I would have to take it.

—TINA TURNER, *rock star*

Life is like being at the dentist. You always think that the worst is still to come, and yet it's over already.

—OTTO VON BISMARCK, *German statesman*

The problem is not your choice, the problem is how you live with that choice. So the answer, stay or leave, turns on whether you think you can change.

—PETER D. KRAMER, *psychiatrist*

I'll never divorce him—how can I, he's a divorce lawyer—but I may just shoot him.

—ERICA JONG, *novelist*

I saw myself getting to the end of my life and wondering what it would have been like if I had dared to take a chance and live a life for which I had no plan. I told my husband "no."

—SANDRA HURTES, *writer*

A friend told me, "I knew that divorce was pending when she started to introduce me as her first husband."

—MIKE ROCHMAN, *sales rep*

"Congratulations or Condolences?"

Breaking the News

Telling others about your divorce is uncomfortable for them. People don't know what to say: "Do I offer congratulations or condolences?"

You can say, "We're separating and (a) I had to ask him/her to leave; (b) I was as surprised as you are; (c) it was a hard decision but a mutual one; or (d) !*&#)!!**@!$!"

—VICKI LANSKY, *nonfiction writer*

Miss Manners used to say [about an impending divorce]: "Oh, I am so sorry," until a lady replied, "If I'm happy and he's happy, what are you so sorry about?" Miss Manners was forced to acknowledge that a quiet "I wish you the best" is more appropriate.

—JUDITH MARTIN, *Miss Manners*

Your divorce presents a crisis for your friends, too. Not only are they threatened in their own marriages but they get trapped in the hall of mirrors of your divorce. They don't know what to believe, how to comfort you, or whom to ask to dinner.

—ABIGAIL TRAFFORD, *journalist*

The lady with all the answers does not know the answers to this one.

—ANN LANDERS, revealing her own marital breakup in her advice column

Divorcism is like any other prejudice—an unreal expectation caused by lack of knowledge.

—CONSTANCE AHRONS, *therapist*

Nothing whets our appetite quite so much as the dissolution of those marriages that had seemed, on the surface, perfect. The unpleasant secrets, we feel, were more hidden, more closely guarded, buried deeper and therefore more valuable and more satisfying to exhume.

—FRANCINE PROSE, *novelist*

Always tell the truth. It will please some people and astonish the rest.

—MARK TWAIN, *humorist*

You find that when you are getting divorced, people tell you things. They know you are suffering and think you will understand. Their private miseries and secret longings will be safe with you.

—ABIGAIL TRAFFORD, *journalist*

I was more worried about telling my parents than I was about telling my husband because here was their pride and joy disappointing them by leaving their son-in-law.

—PENNY KAGANOFF, *editor and journalist*

Don't break up in a restaurant. If they want to cry or rage, you don't want an audience. It's hard enough to break up without an audience.

—ROBIN GORMAN NEWMAN, *relationship expert*

He called me for a divorce on the phone. He said, "This will only take a minute."

—ANGIE DICKINSON, *actor,* on composer Burt Bacharach

Sure, it's bad to be dumped, but sometimes it can be worse to do the dumping. Those who have been let go can at least wallow in self-pity, or erupt in righteous anger. They get the sympathy; people buy them dinner.

—EDWARD LEWINE, *writer*

I was doing the *Cher* show, and I was pregnant and the only one who knew it. My press agent called me up and said, "Cher, do you know Gregory's divorcing you?" And I said, without pausing, "No, hum a few bars."

—CHER, *actor and singer,* on her second divorce, from rock star Greg Allman

I think you need to commit as much energy to the end of the relationship as you did to the beginning. We are so bad with endings in our culture. Everything comes to an end.

—ANNIE SPRINKLE, *porn actress and prostitute turned performance artist*

One may radiate quiet happiness, but that all-out triumphant air is not in good taste.

—JUDITH MARTIN, *Miss Manners*

"The Friend Who Stands By You"

The Network of Support

One of the most important factors in your public divorce is the Friend Who Stands By You. Sometimes it's a new friend you meet after the marriage is over; sometimes it's a friend from childhood who knew you before you were married; rarely is it a friend who knew you both well.

—ABIGAIL TRAFFORD, *journalist*

Your married friends avert their eyes if they run into you and do not invite you for dinner, because they figure losing is contagious. Besides, you might cry. You will not, but never mind.

—MARY CANTWELL, *journalist*

Women have, on average, six friends with whom they regularly talk and share intimacies. Most married men say they have one: their wife.

—JOHN STOSSEL, *TV interviewer*

Only to a chemist is blood always thicker than water. At times of grief, good friends can be better than bad relations. Let in only people who will boost you, not sap you.

—Joan Rivers, *comedian*

It is reasonable to expect a friend to come through in a crisis. It is not reasonable to expect her to disrupt her whole life. Even the best of mothers, upon watching her child fall for the first time, will check to look for bruises, perhaps giving the child a hand so that she may regain her balance. As for doing the walking, well, that's up to the child.

—Eva Margolies, *therapist*

At one point, the telling of my divorce story ran almost 90 minutes without commercial interruption and not once did my best phone friend ask me to fast-forward to the juicy parts.

—Victoria Register, *high-school English teacher*

I went home for comfort, but when I cried, my father said, "I sure as hell wouldn't want to be married to you." That ended two relationships at once.

—Rebecca Platzner, *children's librarian*

Divorcing couples deserve the same amount of loving support in starting a new life that they received when they were first married.

—JEROME A. PRICE, *family therapist*

I couldn't have made it without my sister. Talking to friends was like going public, but with my sister it was safe, it was private, and a lifeline for us both.

—*Anonymous college student*

Who's gonna get custody of our friends?

—SANDRA R. MURPHY, *matrimonial lawyer*

A Roman divorced from his wife, being highly blamed by his friends, who demanded, "Was she not chaste? Was she not fair? Was she not fruitful?" holding out his shoe, asked them whether it was not new and well made. "Yet," added he, "none of you can tell where it pinches me."

—PLUTARCH, *biographer,* in *Life of Aemilius Paulus*

All my friends are doing it, and quite frankly, I feel left out. Woman 37, never married. Seeks divorce. POB 655.

—*Parody of a personal ad on the Internet*

He smiled. "This isn't meant to upset you, because I like you, Bill, and I would never try to upset a friend, but it's going to be awful, it's going to be so awful you can't believe it, you'll be wishing it was only a nightmare before you're through, it's the worst experience of your adult life, I promise you, I know, I'm your friend, I've been through it twice and ended up with nothing, just ashes, Bill, you'll be wishing for death before it's done."

He went on and on, smiling, and all I could think of was what would he have said if he'd been trying to upset me?

—WILLIAM GOLDMAN, *screenwriter and novelist*

"Parent-ectomies"

For the Sake of the Children

You would never consider performing an appendectomy on a child without anesthetic, but we do "parent-ectomies" on kids every day.

—Frank Williams, *psychiatrist*

My parents stayed together for the sake of the children. When the children were grown and settled, my parents divorced—for their own sake. Nothing is so shocking, somehow, as news you've been half-expecting all your life.

—Walter Kirn, *critic*

To adults, divorce is a solution; to their children it's the problem.

—Richard Peck, *novelist*

Divorces don't wreck children's lives. People do.

—Vicki Lansky, *nonfiction writer*

A good divorce does not require that parents share child-care responsibilities equally. It means that they share them clearly.

—Constance Ahrons, *therapist*

You owe your children a great deal, but the number-one thing you owe them is a happy parent. Think of your own future while you are thinking of theirs.

—Mary Rogers, *financial counselor*

Begotten and born most often in love, children are living proof after divorce of love gone wrong, consistent reminders of the broken promises of marriage.

—Linda Bird Francke, *writer*

Kids grieve, their lives are reduced to a commodity to be sliced up like pizza, and their parents battle over the highest of stakes. [But] there's one big plus to divorces that involve children: kids are incontrovertible evidence that the marriage was not a mistake.

—Ashton Applewhite, *writer*

All single-parent families do not come in one flavor—weak. There are as many varieties as among two-parent families.

—Ellen Goodman, *columnist*

There are many things children accept as "grown-up things" over which they have no control and for which they have no responsibility. Parents who are separating really need to help their children put divorce on that grown-up list, so that children do not see themselves as the cause of their parents' decision to live apart.

—FRED ROGERS, *children's television personality*

"What happened with Daddy and me, it had nothing to do with you," I said. It's what we're supposed to say, isn't it, whenever a marriage is ripped apart and the kids come tumbling out, tumbling down? And I don't know why, because it's such a big, bold-faced lie that any kid with half a brain could figure out.

—ANNA QUINDLEN, *novelist,* in *Black and Blue*

Children who grow up seeing their parents run away from home have a different relationship with marriage than those who saw parents hang in there. Brutal marriages may be bad for children, but I'm not sure boring marriages are.

—FRANK PITTMAN, *psychiatrist*

A child is very disturbed when the relationship between his parents is very disturbed. Divorce is not the costliest experience for a child. Unhappy marriage without divorce can be far more destructive.

—J. LOUISE DESPERT, *child psychiatrist*

With divorce, adolescents feel abandoned, and they are angry at both parents for letting them down. Often they feel that their parents broke the rules and so now they can, too.

—MARY PIPHER, *psychologist*

My brain seems irreparably divided into Mom's side and Dad's side. And the question of whether I'm thankful that my parents stayed married so long for my sake seems insoluble. Sometimes I wish they'd split when I was young and introduced me to modern chaos earlier.

—WALTER KIRN, *critic*

I do not argue that children have no chance of health or happiness after divorce, but that they have severe emotional challenges to meet.

—JUDITH WALLERSTEIN, *social researcher*

When a marriage is going well, and your child has traits that remind you of your spouse, those traits endear the child to you. When a marriage is going badly, or there's been a divorce, the traits of your child that remind you of your spouse are the traits most likely to irritate or enrage you.

—JOSEPH TELUSHKIN, *rabbi and writer*

I figured if I was bad enough [at age 9], both my parents would have to come to the principal's office. It was me bringing them back together again.

—JENNIFER ANISTON, *actor*

Every time my father would remarry, my new stepmother would tell me, "You'll always have a room here." Well, I'm still waiting for my room.

—PETER FONDA, *actor,* at age 42

Perhaps, like serial monogamy in robins, foxes, and other species that mate only for a breeding season, the human pair bond originally evolved to last long enough to raise a single child through infancy. The seven-year-itch, recast as a four-year human reproductive cycle, may be a biological phenomenon.

—HELEN E. FISHER, *anthropologist*

Try not to get divorced.

—MARY CATE WALKER, age 8, in *The 11th Commandment: Wisdom from Our Children*

It's funny how both my children made friends with new kids after their dad moved out, kids who, like them, had a different address and phone number for the mom and the dad. Life does get normal again. A new normal.

—BARBARA DIAMOND GOLDIN, *children's book writer*

You don't have to be abused or betrayed to have a bad marriage—a marriage that cannot be fixed, even with the help of all the therapists on the Upper West Side, or all the preachers in Louisiana. And a bad marriage is no good for children. Just ask the adults who grew up in one.

—KATHA POLLITT, *columnist*

To label a child whose parents have separated as being from a "broken home" is unfortunate and unnecessary. Very little gets broken that can't be mended over time.

—JANET MALLEY, *social researcher*

My father left, and like a table short a leg, things had been out of whack ever since.

—SARAH DESSEN, *novelist,* in *That Summer*

A witty woman I know says that when lovers break up, getting over it takes about as long again as the pair were in love. But when children are involved, I wonder if the breakup of parents may not instead take about as long to get over as the age of the children when the breach occurred.

—ALIX KATES SHULMAN, *novelist*

So he says he wants his family back. His family never left; he did.

—ERZSI DEAK, *writer*

Most children do not give up on their biological fathers, even if they are ne'er-do-wells who have abandoned them without a backward glance.

—Judith Wallerstein and Sandra Blakeslee, *social researchers*

Today my name is *Sorrow.* But write and tell my father, on the day of his returning, *Joy* shall be my name.

—Giuseppe Giacosa and Luigi Illica, *librettists* for
Giacomo Puccini's opera, *Madama Butterfly*

A man with a child he never sees is an amputee. He walks through life with a limb missing, a chronic ache.

—Dani Shapiro, *novelist,* in *Picturing the Wreck*

A whole new life opened for her which was dramatic and glorious and romantic and marvelous. Well, that was grand for Mother. But I didn't happen to live with the part that was glorious; I was left with what was left. I was part of what was left.

—Pia Lindstrom, age 17, about her mother, actor Ingrid Bergman

Many divorced fathers feel abused by the courts—which still decide custody cases in the mother's favor 90 percent of the time—and resent being used as a paycheck when they have no say in the child's life.

—Mark Bryan, the Father Project

It's unnatural to *visit* your son. God, it's hard.

—ELLIOTT GOULD, *actor,* divorced from singer and director Barbra Streisand

The issue is not whether parents without custody have an impact on their children's lives, but whether their impact is positive or negative.

—GENEVIEVE CLAPP, *divorce mediator*

It sometimes seems as if divorce changes husband and wife into brother and sister, competitive siblings. Their child, or children, is the single bottle of Coca-Cola they are splitting equally, each panicked the other will get more.

—DELIA EPHRON, *writer*

It helps if you can think of [coparenting after a hostile divorce] as a business relationship. In business, you don't even have to *like* your partner.

—CARRIE FRIED SUTTON, *psychologist*

But Daddy Said I Could is a preferred game for children of divorce, since they generally see only one parent at a time, and can elaborate upon the old divide-and-conquer routine that they played during the marriage.

—MEL KRANTZLER, *therapist*

For a couple with young children, divorce seldom comes as a "solution" to stress, only as a way to end one form of pain and accept another.

—FRED ROGERS, *children's television personality*

Forget dating. Forget striking a balance between work and family. Most single parents report that discipline is by far the toughest issue.

—JEAN CALLAHAN, *journalist*

One of the most serious obligations of each of the divorced parents is never by word or act to express scorn, contempt, or disrespect for the other to one of the children of the marriage.

—ELEANOR ROOSEVELT, *human rights activist and American First Lady*

The stepparent often provokes intense jealousy and resentment. After all, it isn't the children who fell in love with this outsider or gave this interloper permission to take up half of the true parent's attention.

—BENJAMIN SPOCK, *pediatrician*

When they were living with Mom, it was, "You're my best buddy." Then along comes Prince Charming and the child all of a sudden has to go to bed on time.

—ELIZABETH McGONAGLE, *social worker*

"Step" was given a bad name by the publicity attached to the unfortunate home life of Cinderella. Many kind people who devote their lives to children they didn't foist upon the world resent the name of stepmother or stepfather, which suggests that they hand out poisoned apples.

—JUDITH MARTIN, *Miss Manners*

The wonderful thing about my stepchildren is that they aren't quite as sure as my birth child that I will love them, no matter what. They try harder. And, come to think of it, so do I.

—ELLEN HOWARD, *children's book writer*

One could argue that a really mature and healthy mother would appreciate that a stepmother can provide her children with many gratifications and that three loving adults are better than two. I myself have not met such women.

—RICHARD A. GARDNER, *child psychiatrist*

I'm sorry to hear that your marriage has gone on the rocks, but most marriages ought to.

—GRACE HEMINGWAY, 1927 letter to her novelist son, Ernest, on the first of his three divorces

When a son or daughter's marriage looks as though it is headed for divorce, parents naturally want to do whatever they can to find quick, simple solutions to complex problems. You might think of it like taking a Crock-Pot recipe and trying to zap it to completion in the microwave. Even a novice cook knows it just won't work!

—THOMAS WHITEMAN, *divorce counselor,* and DEBBIE BARR, *journalist*

Who is the better parent? There is no answer to such a question. If you think there is, be assured it is probably not you.

—VICKI LANSKY, *nonfiction writer*

"Strange and Terrible Behavior"

Anger and Depression

The worst thing about divorce is not what the other person does to you, or how he behaves, but the strange and terrible behavior divorce produces in your own self.

—JOYCE MAYNARD, *writer*

How terrible we feel to be walking around thinking dark thoughts about someone we used to *sleep with*.

—ELLEN GILCHRIST, *novelist*

Hell hath no fury like a brunette replaced by a blonde.

—VICTORIA REGISTER, *high-school English teacher*

I think of my wife, and I think of Lot,
And I think of the lucky break he got.

—WILLIAM COLE, *poet and anthologist,* "Marriage Couplet"

Ashes fly back into the face of the one who throws them.

—*Nigerian proverb*

To tell the truth, it's the face that he loves, not the wife. Let three wrinkles appear, let her skin dry out and sag a little, let her teeth grow dingy and her eyes shrink. "Pack your bags," a flunky will say, "and get out. You're a nuisance to us now, and you blow your nose too much. Get out, right away, hurry up. Another woman is coming with a dry nose."

—JUVENAL, *Roman poet,* translated by Paul Pascal

I gave my beauty and my youth to men. . . . What attracts me most in a man is his absence.

—BRIGITTE BARDOT, *actor,* divorced three times

In my next life, I want you to come back as a woman, and I as a man. I'll marry you. Then you'll know how I suffer.

—CHEN SAO BING, *watercolorist,* when leaving her husband

I was served her affidavit. Yes, of course,
I could have known she'd dredge up that,
    and that.
But such vehemence over the incident with
    the cat!
Revelation is the essence of divorce.

—DAVID CURZON, *poet,* in "Divorce"

Bloody hell . . . I can't stand the confines of this marriage. [Charles] makes my life real torture.

—PRINCESS DIANA on her marriage to Prince Charles

A bloody awful mistake.

—PRINCE CHARLES on his marriage to Princess Diana

Hatred binds us to its object as mercilessly as does love. Forgive and move on, or stay angry and remain stuck.

—ELIZABETH HICKEY, *social worker*

It is easier to forgive when the offending partner becomes ill and almost pitiful.

—DIANA SIMON, *librarian*

We'll work out the property settlement amicably—with guns and knives.

—HAROLD ROBBINS, *novelist*

Most couples start out arguing about one thing and, within five minutes, are arguing about the way they are arguing.

—JOHN GRAY, *relationship expert*

Don José and the Donna Inez led
For some time an unhappy sort of life,
Wishing each other, not divorced, but dead;
They lived respectably as man and wife,
Their conduct was exceedingly well-bred,
And gave no outward signs of inward strife,
Until at length the smother'd fire broke out,
And put the business past all kind of doubt.

—LORD BYRON, *poet Don Juan,* Canto I, XXVI

An older relative of mine used to say she thought spiders had the right idea. They ate their mates when they were finished with them!

—ELLEN HOWARD, *children's book writer*

It could have been a lot worse. They could have sentenced me to spend the rest of my life with Martha Mitchell.

—JOHN MITCHELL, *Attorney General,* on his 1975 Watergate conviction and his marriage to Martha Mitchell

Where society insists on making the bonds of relationships almost unbreakable, by difficult divorce or rigorous convention, then it is small wonder that a number of quietly spoken, patient people go out to buy arsenic on the flimsy pretext of putting down rats, or killing dandelions, or merely improving their complexions.

—JOHN MORTIMER, *attorney and novelist*

There are only about twenty murders a year in London and not all are serious—some are just husbands killing their wives.

—G. H. HATHERILL, *Commander of Scotland Yard,* 1954

My wife is a killer. She dreams at night of my death.

—JOHN UPDIKE, *novelist,* in *Toward the End of Time*

I'm not upset about my divorce. I'm only upset I'm not a widow.

—ROSEANNE, *comedian,* on her second divorce, from actor Tom Arnold

Fortunately we're not tried on our unconscious wishes, or we should all be in jail.

—DIANA TRILLING, *critic*

They clinked their glasses. "To us," Elise said. "To the First Wives."
Annie smiled. "Can our motto be *'We don't get mad, we just get even'*?"
"Oh, please," begged Brenda, "can't we do both?"

—OLIVIA GOLDSMITH, *novelist,* in *The First Wives Club*

Divorce is a kind of killing, you know. The principal parties murder whatever they had known together, effectively reducing memory and desire to ashes.

—ED McBAIN, *novelist,* in *Mary Mary*

The prefix UN took over my life: unloved, unmarried, unattractive, unhappy, uncomfortable, unrecognizable, unglued, undone, unreal.

—DONNA D'AMICO MAYER, *psychiatric nurse*

After every divorce someone will be running like a cat, tin cans tied to its tail: spooked and slowed down.

—ANNE ROIPHE, *novelist*

One of the worst things I had to contend with was living with things we had acquired together. I was all set to forget about him, and up would bob an old chair, and I could see him sitting in it. My God, it was ghastly!

—BETTE DAVIS, *actor,* about the first of four husbands

It's better to be a fake at happiness than an honest depressive.

—JOAN RIVERS, *comedian*

It's like
when you come home
& for some reason
the electricity
has been turned off,

& everytime
you enter the bedroom
or the kitchen,
you automatically
flick on the light switch,

then you look up
& you feel silly
because
you remember
there's no electricity.

It's like that,
sort of. . . . .

—LOUIS PHILLIPS, *poet,* "Separation & Divorce, ii"

The State of Vermont sent me a registered letter saying they would dissolve my marriage if I signed the enclosed papers. Dissolve. Throw four years of your life in a glass of water and watch it fizz away like Alka-Seltzer.

—WALLY LAMB, *novelist,* in *She's Come Undone*

Coming out of a broken marriage, you feel like half a pair of scissors. The edge is sharp, but you can't cut with it.

—ABIGAIL TRAFFORD, *journalist*

I had been living alone five months when Thanksgiving rolled around and exploded in my face. I drowned myself in memories that day, and for more than one moment I had a wild urge to call my ex-wife and say, "Let's try it again." Each time, however, reality would raise its ugly head, and I would be thrown back on my grief.

—MEL KRANTZLER, *therapist*

Because of the divorce, I haven't had time to eat as much. Panic attacks will do it. You just suffer and stop eating. But I wouldn't recommend the Divorce Diet.

—PATRICIA RICHARDSON, *actor*

Beware not only of the bottle, but of the telephone, which many people reach for with the same desperation, and overuse with the same self-indulgence and sloppiness.

—JUDITH MARTIN, *Miss Manners*

Nothing in the universe can travel at the speed of light, they say, forgetful of the shadow's speed.

—HOWARD NEMEROV, *poet*

Their separation and divorce did not feel like good freedom to her, it felt like being thrown out of the igloo in the middle of a snowstorm. There is lots of space to wander in, but it's all cold.

—MARILYN FRENCH, *novelist,* in *The Women's Room*

The day had the hurried, rancid flavor of a backstreet abortion or a high-stakes cockfight, and it left an imprint of deep personal shame.

—MIA FARROW, *actor,* on her quick Mexican divorce from singer Frank Sinatra

I feel as obliterated as a figure erased from a blackboard. Life stands still. I have nothing. I *am* nothing. What do I do at age forty-nine—go out on the nearest street corner and announce my new status?

—BARBARA MALLEY, *writer*

The overturned canoe syndrome: Imagine a person paddling a canoe through choppy water, struggling to stay afloat. Suddenly a large wave overturns the canoe. The person *could* swim to shore, but is so depleted from the previous struggle that she sinks.

—CAROL TRAVIS, *social psychologist*

I barely slept, some nights, even though I was exhausted—a terrible vigilance and watchfulness took over, and it was as though I had to stay awake to guard against any other awful things that might happen.

—Donna D'Amico Mayer, *psychiatric nurse*

Getting on with it, putting the problem behind you, is what men are trained to do. When a marriage that is meaningful ends, what is needed is not to just do something but to sit there with the guilt and grief—to mourn and learn and begin to atone.

—Ted Solotaroff, *editor*

In the depth of winter, I finally learned that within me there lay an invincible summer.

—Albert Camus, *novelist*

Feelings of helplessness are common to every woman I have talked to who either leaves or is left by her husband. And I am told it is even worse for men. I love the apocryphal story of the newly divorced man wheeling his cart through the supermarket in a daze, who finally asks for help, "Where will I find the toast?"

—Mary Tyler Moore, *actor*

Dividing up Hopes and Memories

Lawyers, Money, and Possessions

To divide up property is to divide up hopes and memories as well.

—MARY ROGERS, *financial consultant*

It is better to have loved and lost, but only if you have a good lawyer.

—HERB CAEN, *columnist*

A man I talked to this morning, I've done three divorces for. Give 'em a nice divorce, they keep coming.

—RAOUL LIONEL FELDER, *divorce attorney*

It's better to send your own kids to college than your lawyer's.

—STEPHEN ERICKSON, *divorce mediator*

It takes a certain amount of intelligence to know when you've run into a blank wall; most people prefer to bang their heads against it and then hire a lawyer to explain to them that it can't be moved.

—A. B. YEHOSHUA, *novelist,* in *A Late Divorce*

People run up enormous legal fees and then complain about the avariciousness of all lawyers. It does no good to tell them that a lawyer's time is money, and that an hour of haggling over a frying pan costs as much as an hour's discussion of a life insurance policy.

—MEL KRANTZLER, *therapist*

The lawyer's first obligation should be to make peace, not money.

—WALTER L. KANTROWITZ, *attorney,* and HOWARD EISENBERG, *writer*

The purpose of no-fault is to take the acrimony out of matrimony.

—HERBERT GLIEBERMAN, *divorce attorney*

The legal profession created a new beast: not *no-fault,* but *unilateral* divorce. Today, while it still takes two to marry, it takes only one to divorcee.

—MAGGIE GALLAGHER, *journalist*

The great misconception is that divorce laws change people's behavior. People's behavior changes divorce laws.

—ANDREW CHERLIN, *sociologist*

Divorce law reforms were a response to the rising incidence of divorce rather than the cause of it.

—RODERICK PHILLIPS, *divorce historian*

Take comfort in the thought that, though there are seldom any winners in a divorce, there needn't be any losers.

—ESTHER BERGER, *investment adviser*

Mediation is like the difference between buying a suit off the rack and having one custom-made.

—H. JAY FOLBERG, *professor of law*

Mediation is a transformative process where the powerless and humiliated party can recapture his or her dignity. Finding a solution proves they *can* run their own life. It's about recovering your soul.

—BRIAN MULDOON, *divorce mediator*

Mediation becomes a form of coercion, emphasizing means over ends, harmony over justice, and efficiency over due process.

—CONSTANCE AHRONS, *therapist*

Mediation is great when it works, but it requires three cool and mutually committed heads, and few couples on the brink of civil war can summon up the necessary detachment or collaborative spirit.

—ASHTON APPLEWHITE, *writer*

Marriage is one of the few contracts in which the law explicitly protects the defaulting party at the expense of his or her partner. The one who leaves, wins.

—MAGGIE GALLAGHER, *journalist*

Paper napkins never return from a laundry, nor love from a trip to the law courts.

—JOHN BARRYMORE, *actor*

Some lawyers say they find negotiating [prenuptial] agreements more depressing than handling divorces, where at least the bitterness has grown from experience, not from anticipation.

—JULIE SALAMON, *writer*

I got all dressed up in my black dress and long gloves. I was so conscious of this very serious, adult thing I was about to do, going to lawyer's office to talk about getting a divorce. I felt like I was going to a funeral.

—LONI ANDERSON, *actor,* before the first of three divorces

Lawyers are called in to pick clean the corpses. The death has occurred much earlier.

—Erica Jong, *novelist,* in *How to Save Your Own Life*

A lawyer is never entirely comfortable with a friendly divorce, any more than a good mortician wants to finish his job and then have the patient sit up on the table.

—Jean Kerr, *playwright*

Generally a divorce lawyer would like a stupid rich woman. A stupid *compliant* rich woman.

—Raoul Lionel Felder, *divorce lawyer*

I watch her [in court], and as a character in a novel she's delicious, but in real life she's a monster.

—Saul Bellow, *novelist,* about his third wife, whose alimony and fraud suits lasted more than 20 years

You don't know anything about a woman until you meet her in court.

—Norman Mailer, *novelist,* divorced five times

You never really know a man until you have divorced him.

—Zsa Zsa Gabor, *actor,* divorced eight times

I played Santa Claus many times, and if you don't believe it, check out the divorce settlements awarded my wives.

—GROUCHO MARX, *comedian,* married three times

When a woman faces actually going it alone, a link between "unmarried" and "destitute" keeps surfacing like an annoying car alarm. It's probably not being stolen and it's certainly not your car, but it keeps waking you up.

—ASHTON APPLEWHITE, *writer*

Alimony is the most exorbitant of all stud-fees, and the worst feature of it is that you pay it retroactively.

—JOHN BARRYMORE, *actor*

In love, you pay as you leave.

—MARK TWAIN, *humorist*

Only the rich plan for divorce even as they get married. The rest of us, like criminals who refuse to think about prison in the midst of their felonies, never do. It would incapacitate us.

—JOHN TAYLOR, *writer*

Like nannies, second homes, and plastic surgery—formerly the exclusive province of the very rich—prenuptial agreements are increasingly being sought by young professional people.

—JULIE SALAMON, *writer*

Equitable distribution: he kept the diamond mine, she got the shaft.

—OLIVIA GOLDSMITH, *novelist,* in *The First Wives Club*

Money is like a sixth sense, without which you cannot make use of the other five.

—W. SOMERSET MAUGHAM, *novelist*

[With a prenuptial agreement] the less powerful person—usually the woman—ends up feeling that she was coerced and that the marriage was conditional. The underlying resentment and mistrust never get completely resolved.

—LINDA CARTER, *couples therapist*

I never saw a prenuptial agreement yet that didn't wind up in a divorce.

—MARVIN MITCHELSON, *palimony lawyer*

The truth is, I hate the concept of a prenuptial contract, but that doesn't mean it's not necessary. It's for my own peace of mind.

—DONALD TRUMP, *business mogul,* before his second marriage, to Marla Maples

"This wasn't a marriage," a friend of mine said, referring to the Trumps. "This was a lease with an option to buy."

—JULIE SALAMON, *writer*

Testosterone is the key element in moneymaking, and also moneykeeping, which is just as important. So I think it's basically a boys' game and they'll always win. Consequently, women will simply have to content themselves with not having to play football in high school—a more than fair trade.

—FRAN LEBOWITZ, *humorist*

The difference between divorce and legal separation is that a legal separation gives a husband time to hide his money.

—JOHNNY CARSON, *TV host,* divorced three times

My friend once said to me that every divorce ends with a fight over who gets the side table. Mine was no different: I didn't get it.

—CLAIRE BLOOM, *actor,* about her divorce from novelist Philip Roth

The lawyer had us make lists of our stuff. Chuck said he felt bad that there were so many more things on his list than on mine. He'd only just noticed that everything had been for him.

—REBECCA PLATZNER, *children's librarian*

He lost his wife, but kept his car. He'd rather lose five wives than his XKE.

—OLIVIA GOLDSMITH, *novelist,* in *The First Wives Club*

Eighty to 90 percent of men wind up, within three or four years, better off financially than they ever were before. Just the opposite is true for women.

—SORRELL TROPE, *family-law specialist*

Over $10 million, the husband will make an offer that's considerably less than half. The general feeling is, "What's she going to do with all that money?"

—DEE SAMUELS, *matrimonial attorney*

He brought home the bacon, but I shopped for it, cooked it, and cleaned up after it.

—LORNA J. WENDT, on why she deserves the $20 million she received after her divorce from General Electric executive Gary Wendt

Lorna Wendt just didn't think of the family property as "his" to "give," but rather "theirs" to share. From her point of view, she was part of a team.

—SARAH OLDHAM, *attorney*

She got more of the emotional rewards of the marriage, and I got more of the material rewards.

—GARY WENDT, *business mogul*

I can turn it around and say, "Well, what does *he* need all that money for?" He's out there working and I've been fired.

—LORNA J. WENDT, *ex-corporate wife*

You can't have everything. Where would you put it?

—STEVEN WRIGHT, *comedian*

Divorce may be a contact sport, but it need not be played under the rules of extreme fighting.

—LOIS BRENNER, *divorce lawyer*

Divorce is an expensive proposition and the specter of contributing to the upkeep of two homes may be the major reason why there aren't more divorces than there are.

—RICHARD A. GARDNER, *child psychiatrist*

Why do Hollywood divorces cost so much? Because they're worth it.

—JOHNNY CARSON, *TV host*

"To Release and Forgive"

New Rituals and Ancient Wisdom

A reversal of the marriage ritual: Vows to release and forgive one another replace the traditional wedding vows to honor and cherish. As an ending to the ceremony, the couple then give back their wedding rings, placing them in their exspouse's right hand.

—CONSTANCE AHRONS, *therapist*

Marriage begins officially with a ceremony, usually a religious one and always one that is in keeping with the requirements of civil law. Divorce, which is an equally serious event, is customarily a lonely time. The day the final decree is granted, the individuals come away empty-handed and unloved.

—FLORENCE W. KASLOW, *therapist*

Why not a divorce modeled after a raucous New Orleans funeral? There would be mournful music played on the way to the ceremony, and upbeat, high-stepping jazz afterward. Each spouse in turn, when asked whether they wished to continue to be married to the other, could respond, "I don't!" The minister could conclude the ceremony by saying, "I now pronounce you man and woman."

—Jerome A. Price, *family therapist*

Another wedding ring ritual was developed by an artist [who] totes a sledgehammer to carefully set up parties at which the newly separated may bash the most symbolic memento of their marriage.

—Constance Ahrons, *therapist*

I have had some unhappily married couples melt down their wedding rings and forge them into new ones to symbolize their commitment to a fresh start; divorced couples who must bring up their children together could use this ring ritual to represent the beginning of a new kind of relationship.

—Jerome A. Price, *family therapist*

We create cakes for all occasions, including divorces. Sometimes a divorce is a happy thing and people want to celebrate their freedom. Or someone may purchase a cake to help cheer up someone who is going through a difficult breakup. This cake is usually the total opposite of a wedding cake. Usually it's a one-tier cake simply decorated and inscribed "Happy Divorce," "Good Riddance," or "Here's to the Future."

—MARIA SANCHEZ, *owner of Sweet Maria's bakery*

You know, if there was a nice ceremony like getting married for divorce, it'd be much better.

—JOHN LENNON, *singer and composer*

When a man takes a woman and marries her, and it comes to pass that she find no favor in his eyes, because he has found something unseemly in her, let him write her a bill of divorcement, and give it into her hand, and send her out of his house.

—Deuteronomy 24:1

And the twain shall be one flesh; so then they are no more twain, but one flesh. What therefore God hath joined together, let no man put asunder.

—Mark 10:8–9

But I say unto you, that whosoever shall put away his wife, saving for the cause of fornication, causeth her to commit adultery; and whosoever shall marry her that is divorced committeth adultery.

—Matthew 5:32

It is better to marry than to burn.

—I Corinthians 7:9

The law of God permitted divorce for the help of human weakness. Let not the remedy be despised.

—PAULUS FAGIUS, *Bible scholar*

Judaism discourages loneliness, but it also realizes that a bad marriage can be worse than being alone. Thus Jewish divorce, when necessary, is condoned.

—MAURICE LAMM, *rabbi*

Jewish law regards divorce, not as a punishment for a crime, but simply as the frank admission of a failure. The grounds upon which a divorce is issued are therefore not limited to adultery.

—ROBERT GORDIS, *professor of Biblical studies*

If a man divorces his first wife, even the altar sheds tears.

—Talmud, B. Gittin 90b

A *get* [Jewish religious divorce] is particularly demeaning for women because the Jewish laws that consecrate marriage and divorce also subjugate women to a passive role in these essential life rituals.

—PENNY KAGANOFF, *editor and journalist*

My ex-husband, on the eve of his second marriage, phoned to ask if I'd be willing to submit to an Orthodox Jewish divorce to satisfy his new wife's family. Apparently each jurisdiction required its own particular form of hocus-pocus; but whether the magic words appeared in English, Spanish, or Aramaic, sanctified by a judge, *abogado,* or *rebbe* made no difference to me, as long as they left me free.

—ALIX KATES SHULMAN, *political activist and writer*

You will never be able to deal justly between wives however much you desire [to do so]. But [if you have more than one wife] do not turn altogether away [from one], leaving her in suspense.

—Qur'an 4:129

[Husband to wife:] I divorce you! I divorce you! I divorce you!

—*Muslim formula of divorce*

Allah likes the house which is inhabited in the wake of marriage and dislikes the house which is abandoned in the wake of divorce. There is nothing more detestable to Allah than a divorce.

—IMAM SADIQ

In some Arab countries, a man could divorce his wife by putting her shoes outside his door. In other cultures a shoe outside the door only signified that the person wanted to be left alone and undisturbed.

—CHARLOTTE and DAVID YUE, *nonfiction writers*

She was my slipper and I cast her off.

—*Bedouin divorce ritual, as the husband removes his shoe*

An annulment is not a divorce. Unlike a divorce, an annulment does not say something has either broken down or ended. It says the marriage never truly existed in the first place.

—SHEILA RAUCH KENNEDY, *city planner*

Of course I think we had a true marriage. But that doesn't matter now. I don't believe this stuff. Nobody actually believes it. It's just Catholic gobbledygook, Sheila. But you just have to say it this way because, well, because that's the way the Church is.

—JOSEPH KENNEDY, *congressman,* on his ex-wife's opposition to an annulment

I felt like I didn't matter, like all that effort and all that time that I spent didn't matter. He wanted me to say that there was never a marriage, and there was a marriage. It failed, but there *was* a marriage.

—BARBARA ZIMMERMAN, *dog handler,* about her husband's request for
an annulment

Annulment is not an easy process, it makes you look squarely at the decisions you have made in life, and assess them with brutal honesty. Like confession, in order to do it well, you must really lay your soul bare. Then it can become a healing balm which allows you to start living your own life.

—VIRGINIA NOREY, *book designer*

The [Catholic] annulment is a fiction, obtained as an adjunct to a hoax. Annulments are the magical product of an incomprehensible process in which legal reasons play no part and clerical discretion is absolute.

—JOHN T. NOONAN, *professor of law and religious studies*

I felt as though [the Catholic church] was about to negate a twenty-three-year career [as a wife and mother]. It's hard to believe in a church that can be hypocritical about this. It's a bunch of celibate old guys deciding what the rest of us are going to do.

—PAT CADIGAN, *writer,* who successfully defended her marriage from
annulment

Even a murderer can seek penance from a priest through confession and be forgiven for his sin. However, a divorced Catholic who has remarried outside the Church cannot even attend confession.

—Sheila Rauch Kennedy, *city planner*

I never felt more sustained by God's mercy and compassion than at this time in my life. The day my annulment was granted, I kept thinking: God has granted me a reprieve! Truly His mercy endures forever.

—Virginia Norey, *book designer*

Sometimes I dream of an eighth sacrament, the sacrament of divorce. Like communion, it is a slim white wafer on the tongue. Like confession, it is forgiveness. Family, friends, God, whoever loves us, forgives us, takes us in again. They are thrilled by our life, our possibilities, our second chances. They weep with gladness that we did not have to die.

—Ann Patchett, *novelist*

"Holding on to the Key"

Moving to a New Home

Holding on to the key is holding onto what now must become one's past. Handing over—or asking for—the key is an important step toward the acceptance of the present. It's important to ask for the key if it has not been forthcoming. Ask, don't demand. If refused, just have your locks changed.

—VICKY LANSKY, *nonfiction writer*

Separation and divorce can be a moving experience, in more ways than one.

—JANE NAHIRNY, *editor*

Is there anything as horrible as starting on a trip? Once you're off, that's all right, but the last moments are earthquake and convulsion, and the feeling that you are a snail being pulled off your rock.

—ANNE MORROW LINDBERGH, *writer*

Through it all, we continued to live in the same apartment. Lawyers tell you to do that. Sometimes it can go that way for years. You probably didn't know this, but if you look up the word "awkward" in the *Oxford English Dictionary,* the first definition reads, "Two divorcing adults living in the same apartment because of legal advice."

—WILLIAM GOLDMAN, *screenwriter and novelist*

I move out for the night or go away for the weekend.

—SARAH FERGUSON, *the Duchess of York,* on what she does when ex-husband Prince Andrew has a date stay at their shared home, Sunninghill

Nothing really sank in until I watched the movers denude the house I lived in for most of my life. And then I sat on the bare floor and stared at the marks on the wall which outlined the places where our furniture used to be. And I cried until I couldn't see those borders anymore.

—*Anonymous 20-year-old male*

Often people don't know why they are so miserable. They can't stop longing for the old place, and they can't seem to engage the new one.

—MINDY THOMPSON FULLILOVE, *psychiatrist*

A few weeks before my last day in the old house, a friend [of my husband] had stopped me on the street and said solicitously, "Moving to a smaller place?" "No," I snapped, "bigger," hating him for his curiosity and distrusting his concern.

—Mary Cantwell, *journalist*

Often a divorce necessitates that the family residence be sold. Even though there is a ceremony of consecration of a new home, there is no ritual of farewell when leaving one's previous home. This suggested benediction can be recited as a family, if that is possible, or individually:

I am grateful for the years of joy and fulfillment that were mine within these walls. The pain of leaving is eased by the memories I shall carry with me and the resolve to fashion another abode where Your presence will prevail.

—Sanford Seltzer, *rabbi*

I am a marvelous housekeeper. Every time I leave a man I keep his house.

—Zsa Zsa Gabor, *actor,* divorced eight times

After 24 years in the "marital residence," moving into my new apartment was petrifying. Everything was different and disorienting: street noises, night sounds, the direct sunlight that didn't arrive till afternoon. Where was the laundry room, the mailbox, the garbage chute? Where was the neighbor who would lend me a hammer? Unnerving . . . but exhilarating, too. *Mine.* This place was my own, mine.

Nine years later, I still come home from work and walk from room to room, taking in the space that marks my new life.

—A. L. Daniels, *editor*

Closing a Door

Looking Back

If one were to give an account of all the doors one has closed and opened, of all the doors one would like to reopen, one would have to tell the story of one's entire life.

—GASTON BACHELARD, *philosopher*

Divorce is a kind of killing, but it cannot kill the memories.

—ED MCBAIN, *novelist,* in *Mary Mary*

A recent study found that divorced men harbor fantasies of a reconciliation a lot longer than women do.

—HUGH DOWNS, *TV host*

For me, the question that most haunts me is not why did you get divorced, but why did you get married?

—ANN HOOD, *novelist*

Most experts agree that recovering from a divorce can take as little as two years, but the average is about four to five years. Some people, however, *never* get over divorce.

—DIANA SHEPHERD, *editor*

The silences are what I remember, not conversations, not even arguments.

—MARY CANTWELL, *journalist*

Separating, it surprised us to discover, left us freer to express ourselves than we had been before. We were no longer paralyzed by the need to preserve the artificial peace. We respected each other's frailties. Separating seemed to bring out the best in both of us.

—JOHN TAYLOR, *writer*

We became quite close working together on the divorce; it was much more our own accomplishment than the wedding had been.

—WILLIAM MEYERS, *novelist,* in *My Life So Far*

It didn't work out that we should be husband and wife. But everybody I ever loved, I still love a little.

—MARILYN MONROE, *actor,* on her marriage to Arthur Miller

All my bad ideas about marriage came from my parents and their disharmony. But all the men I have ever loved, I will love forever.

—JEANNE MOREAU, *actor*

If this was happiness, imagine what the rest of her life had been.

—ORSON WELLES, *film director and actor,* on his marriage to actor Rita Hayworth

I guess the only way to stop divorce is to stop marriage.

—WILL ROGERS, *humorist*

Coupling changes us and so does uncoupling. But in most cases relationships don't end. They change, but they don't end.

—DIANE VAUGHAN, *sociologist*

I learned more about love when Paul and I decided to divorce than I had at any other point in my life. I learned that if friendship is at the core of a relationship, there really isn't any divorce, there's just a change in the form of that relationship.

—PATTI DAVIS, *writer*

I genuinely do not believe in divorce. I know that must sound pretty funny, coming from me.

—ELIZABETH TAYLOR, *actor,* just before the fourth of seven divorces

There remained unresolved questions about the relationships in my life. Was I predestined to repeat these patterns over and over again, like a spider meticulously weaving the same web?

—CLAIRE BLOOM, *actor,* divorced three times

You may think that my giving advice on marriage is like the captain of the *Titanic* giving lessons on navigation.

—JOHNNY CARSON, *TV host,* divorced three times

Happiness is not a life without problems. It's the ability to handle those problems. It took me two marriages—and two divorces—to figure this out.

—MARCIA CLARK, *prosecutor*

We are, all of us, molded and remolded by those who have loved us, and though that love may pass, we remain none the less *their* work—a work that very likely they do not recognize, and which is never exactly what they intended.

—FRANÇOIS MAURIAC, *novelist,* in *The Desert of Love*

When a marriage ends, who is left to understand it?

—JOYCE CAROL OATES, *novelist*

"Not Beloved, but Kin"

Ex-Spouses and Ex-In-Laws

I realized that although my feelings for my ex weren't entirely friendly, he felt like kin. Not beloved, but kin nevertheless.

—Constance Ahrons, *therapist*

It takes a long time to stop loving someone.

—Devlin Kaye, *art director*

Any contact between divorced people somehow smacks of incest; once divorced, the aura of past sexual relations makes further relationship incriminating.

—Margaret Mead, *anthropologist*

There's no fury like an ex-wife searching for a new lover.

—Cyril Connolly, *novelist,* in *The Unquiet Grave*

Mild curiosity is normal, but when you find yourself spending a lot of emotional energy worrying about what he or she is doing (or going out of your way to keep your activities secret from him or her) you are still tied to the past.

—MEL KRANTZLER, *therapist*

"How's your ex-wife?"
"She's divorced, too," he replied.
"That's what we have in common."

—DAVID LEHMAN, *poet,* in "Who She Was"

I found it haunting that the life he was reconstructing seemed to be a mirror image of everything we had done together.

—KATHARINE GRAHAM, *newspaper publisher,* when her husband left her

The wholly unexpected happiness of Larry's second marriage has created within him a new tide of love toward his first wife.

—CAROL SHIELDS, *novelist,* in *Larry's Party*

When we let each other go, it was really an act of love. We helped each other through the divorce and emerged good friends. That was why I didn't hesitate to go to his wedding.

—PATTI DAVIS, *writer*

When there has been no friendship in the marriage, there is no basis for it afterward.

—Constance Ahrons, *therapist*

Not all lesbian ex-lovers become family/friends. Many lesbian breakups can be high-drama and nasty, as acrimonious as the worst straight divorces. In large part, the quality of the lover relationship will determine the quality of the breakup and postlover connection.

—Ellen Shumsky, *psychotherapist*

The ease with which gay men can go from being lovers to just friends is largely dependent upon the kind of divorce they experienced.

—Michael Shernoff, *social worker*

The only thing worse than hearing your ex is remarrying from a third party is actually hearing the news from your ex. It's the last nail in the coffin of what was once your marriage—and your hopes and dreams. If you know anyone whose ex is getting remarried, don't let them spend that day alone. And if you know your ex is getting remarried, don't spend it by yourself.

—Vicky Lansky, *nonfiction writer*

The first time I met my ex-wife's new husband, I was thrilled to see that he was short. A purely sexual response. The fact that I was taller made me the winner.

—JAMES MAHER, *editor*

Your basic extended family today includes your ex-husband or -wife, your ex's new mate, your new mate, possibly your new mate's ex, and any new mate that your new mate's ex has acquired. It consists entirely of people who are not related by blood, many of whom can't stand each other.

—DELIA EPHRON, *writer*

Any ex-wife would say the same thing I did when I first sampled his girlfriend's apple strudel: Ed, you've gotta keep this treasure in the family!

—BARBARA MALLEY, *writer,* who introduced her ex-husband to his second wife

Playing the hangdog role may be socially acceptable, especially to your ex-mother-in-law.

—ABIGAIL TRAFFORD, *journalist*

I said I love her and was sorry for all the crap I said about her. I said, "You're a helluva gal—you just didn't make a good wife for my son."

—JACKIE STALLONE, *mother of actor Sylvester "Sly" Stallone*

If your ex-spouse has healed, he or she will tell the family to stop ostracizing or criticizing you, *and they will.* If it continues, your ex-spouse is either allowing it or encouraging it.

—ANNE N. WALTHER, *therapist*

Family is family to me, no matter what—in fact, when I'm divorced, I always seem to get custody of all the in-laws.

—LONI ANDERSON, *actor,* divorced three times

I don't think it's nice to talk about ex-husbands or ex-wives.

—TAMMY FAYE BAKKER MESSNER, *televangelist*

"Ready to Resume Living"

I'm OK!

Just getting dressed is a signal to yourself that you are ready to resume living. Even if you're going to be home alone, put on makeup, stockings, and jewelry, particularly if you're a woman.

—JOAN RIVERS, *comedian*

Keeping a journal allows a man to tell his psyche that he is serious, that he's willing to listen to his own story. A journal allows time for dealing with his pain, which he could easily ignore by filling his hours with work and diversionary activities.

—JOSEPH JASTRAB, *psychotherapist*

When I first began living by myself, people (most, but not all, well-meaning) kept asking if I was lonely. *Alone* is not *lonely*. I prefer to say, "I'm on my own."

—A. L. DANIELS, *editor*

You can go down, go under—just cave in out of the fear of what it means to be single again. Or you can say this is to open a door that I've never even thought of opening.

—JANE FONDA, *actor and activist*

I realized I would make it when I was driving home from work the other day and I heard the Rolling Stones on the radio. I made a U-turn, headed for a record store, and bought a double CD of the Stones. My husband hated the Rolling Stones.

—DONNA D'AMICO MAYER, *psychiatric nurse*

A kick in the ass is a step forward.

—J. T. O'HARA, *raconteur*

When I got divorced, that was the first time I got to know me.

—SUE ALEXANDER, *children's book writer*

A pair of Nikes helped me revive after the marital meltdown. Two miles, four days a week, cut my Kleenex consumption in half.

—VICTORIA REGISTER, *high-school English teacher*

Although I occasionally cry myself to sleep, I feel like an oppressive weight has been lifted from my life—I've retapped the veins of desire. I wish I could have felt all this as a "wife," but maybe that was an impossible dream.

—Evelyn McDonnell, *writer*

Your lovely wife wants a divorce and you're going to deal with it and eventually heal. Deal and heal.

—Colin Harrison, *novelist,* in *Break and Enter*

In some circles a divorce is carried about as a badge of honor, like going to a psychiatrist.

—Robert Gordis, *professor of Biblical studies*

Life has to be faced: to be rejected; then accepted on new terms with rapture.

—Virginia Woolf, *novelist and essayist*

I live with myself now, not him. I take care of myself—from my own laundry to my soul.

—Susan Spano, *travel writer*

The world breaks everyone and afterward many are strong at the broken places.

—Ernest Hemingway, *novelist,* in *A Farewell to Arms*

Function in disaster, finish in style.

—Lucy Madeira, *educator*

A legal divorce is the definitive outcome of a step-by-step court process. But the emotional recovery from divorce is spiral, not linear.

—Ellie Wymard, *professor of English*

Just before the divorce was final, everyone asked if I was going to change my last name. After 27 years, my last name felt like mine, not his, not his family's. But—most important—I didn't divorce my children. We are strongly connected, always and forever, and our shared name reflects that.

—A. L. Daniels, *editor*

A long time passes between getting a divorce and getting it together.

—Phyllis Gillis, *entrepreneur*

When you can't remember why you hurt, that's when you're healed. When you have to work real hard to re-create the pain, and you can't quite get there, that's when you're better.

—Jane Fonda, *actor and activist*

Finding Your Soul Mate

Dating and Remarriage...
or Not

You may marry a person who is not your soul mate but who will prepare you to find your soul mate eventually. You may have to go through such a marriage, and a divorce, so that you can learn what you have to learn.

—DAVID AARON, *rabbi*

The bed seems a prairie and the sheets still smell of him, and in the supermarket you stick your hand in the meat bin for a roast and withdraw it when you realize that a chop is enough.

—MARY CANTWELL, *journalist*

A single man is an incomplete animal. He resembles the odd half of a pair of scissors.

—BENJAMIN FRANKLIN, *statesman and inventor*

Single girls bring out the mother in everyone, don't you think? Even my dentist is concerned about me.

—"Sheila Farrow" in *The Woman Alone* by PATRICIA O'BRIEN

As a single mother and businesswoman, my juggling act became more difficult. Not long ago, I read an interview with a businesswoman. When asked what she most needed, she responded: a wife. Exactly!

—LILLIAN VERNON, *entrepreneur*

Milk and bread never had a chance to go sour or get moldy in a home with four children. I wondered more than once, how did single people manage to use up food?

—PATRICIA O'BRIEN, *journalist*

I was always either in a relationship or between relationships. I might be between relationships for months at a time, holding open auditions all the while, but that's not the same as being single.

—LAWRENCE BLOCK, *mystery writer*

The after-work hours are the cruelest. Their former wives are catching up on careers; their children are scattered. The weeknight hours between five and nine are now an intimacy void.

—GAIL SHEEHY, *journalist*

It was real hard to be around friends who were couples. Is this the single life? It stinks. I can function. Just don't leave me alone at twilight—that's the loneliest time.

> —PENNY MARSHALL, *actor and director,* after the breakup of a nine-year marriage to director Rob Reiner

I don't think of myself as single . . . or double—I think of myself as a person.

> —SUZANNE NEWTON, *novelist*

Present yourself as a married woman and you are free to indulge in "safe flirting"; present yourself as a divorced woman and you are perceived as a potentially dangerous predator.

> —DAPHNE MERKIN, *essayist*

Sex is the most talked about topic in the singles world, and this is probably very healthy. When we were married, what went on between husband and wife was strictly private, and if you had fears, problems, or unmet needs, you kept them to yourself.

> —CATHERINE NAPOLITANE, *founder of NEXUS, a self-help organization for divorced women*

One person can thread a needle better than two.

> —*African-American proverb*

Whether you're recently separated, long divorced, or a veteran dater, a first date has a kind of back-to-seventh-grade quality about it.

—SANDEE BRAWARSKY, *journalist*

Whenever I date a guy, I think, is this the man I want my children to spend their weekends with?

—RITA RUDNER, *actor*

Middle-aged dating is adolescence all over again. The same fears, same roller coaster of emotions—from boldness to acute embarrassment, elation to degradation, passion to despair.

—GAIL SHEEHY, *journalist*

Call today and see how domesticated Man has become. Who knows. You may never have to cook dinner again.

—*Ad for personal voice introductions for women*

Her personals ad was as much a Situation Wanted as a Help Wanted. Might it be a good idea for each of them to regard their meeting as one in which two peers have exchanged resumés, and have agreed to hire each other? Maybe not.

—SYDNEY BIDDLE BARROWS, *the Mayflower Madam*

Given the high rate of divorce, "better partners" in ever growing numbers are continually coming onto the market.

—DAVID POPENOE, *professor of sociology*

Computer dating? It's terrific if you're a computer!

—RITA MAE BROWN, *novelist*

Think of your date as a potential friend. Then if it ends up being more, that's gravy.

—ANDREA MCGINTY, *founder of "It's Just Lunch," an executive match-making service*

I was never bothered by a man not having any money—in fact, I preferred them not to be stinking rich, as I believed that if a man could buy anything he wanted, it usually meant he thought he could buy me, too.

—JOAN COLLINS, *actor and novelist*

I soon outgrew my need to hide the signposts of time. I had already been married; I had had children; I knew who I was. All of which put me in a position of power. I could choose. If men would eliminate me on the basis of my appearance I would just as readily eliminate them.

—SUSAN DUNDON, *writer*

Getting into a relationship when you're emotionally empty is like going shopping for food when you're hungry: you buy junk.

—BARBARA DE ANGELIS, *relationship expert*

Love does not make the world go round, looking for it does.

—HERB GARDNER, *playwright,* in *Conversations with My Father*

Looking for love with all its catastrophes is a less risky experience than finding it.

—MINA LOY, *poet*

Dating involves several risks: the risk of disappointment, the risk of boredom, the risk of rejection, and the risk of letting some troubled, scary man into your life.

—GAVIN DE BECKER, *security consultant*

You have to be willing to risk rejection, otherwise you won't be able to get involved with anyone. It's like the lottery . . . if you don't play the game, you're not going to meet anyone.

—ROBIN GORMAN NEWMAN, *relationship expert*

The Tarzan approach to coupling makes life easier. Don't let go of one vine until you have the other firmly in hand.

—MARY TYLER MOORE, *actor*

Telling marital war stories is a strong bonding experience for two divorced people, even as early as the first date.

—A. L. Daniels, *editor*

Dating manners for first dates haven't changed. So, *don't* talk about your ex, or your divorce. Don't judge a book by its cover, be rude, be phony, try too hard (or too little), overeat, overdrink, talk on your cell phone, or forget your wallet. And for goodness sake, *don't forget to smile!*

—Andrea McGinty, *founder of "It's Just Lunch," an executive matchmaking service*

Dating isn't what it used to be, but then, maybe it never was.

—Sydney Biddle Barrows, *the Mayflower Madam*

Bookstore pickup line: Have you seen a copy of *Tax Tips for Billionaires*?

—David Letterman, *TV host*

I've found that sex is so much hotter, so much more intense with a new divorcée—especially if the girl in question wasn't all that satisfied with her husband.

—Howard Hughes, *producer and aviator*

Never thank a woman for having sex with you. Your bedroom is not a soup kitchen.

—FLICK EVERETT, *writer*

If you're living a life without sex, you start talking to yourself.

—CAROL SHIELDS, *novelist,* in *Larry's Party*

Two rules for a happy life: no pets with hands, no men with kids.

—FRANCESCA BELANGER, *book designer*

Second marriages can usually be more successful. It's like raising dogs; you just know more the second time around.

—HARRY STACK SULLIVAN, *psychiatrist*

I think it is instinct for a woman to like marriage. I think I shall marry again, but I don't know when.

—ELIZABETH TAYLOR HILTON WILDING TODD FISHER BURTON BURTON WARNER FORTENSKY, *actor,* after the first of eight marriages and seven divorces

Nothing finalizes divorce like remarriage.

—SPARKLE HAYTER, *novelist,* in *Revenge of the Cootie Girls*

When a divorced woman marries a divorced man, four minds inhabit their bed.

—DANIEL ADAMS, *editor*

We got engaged, and eight months later we were married, and we have been idyllically happy ever since. There are a number of reasons why, but there is one factor I'd point to as a *sine qua non*. See, I was ready to be married. The divorce process was complete. I'd finally learned how to be single.

—LAWRENCE BLOCK, *mystery writer*

I love the freedom that I have. I don't have to worry about anybody but myself. I don't have to worry about a man's wardrobe, or his relatives, or his schedule, or his menu, or his allergies. I would not be married again.

—ANN LANDERS, *advice columnist*

I'm not a man who can live alone. I have to think about marriage now.

—ANTHONY QUINN, *actor,* after two divorces, three mistresses, and thirteen children

The extended honeymoon of second marriages: the relief that it is not the first marriage with its particular indignities; the pleasure at one's ability once more to take pleasure with another; the substitution of light opera for grand.

—PETER D. KRAMER, *psychiatrist*

I was embarrassed to be marrying a second time, and for the same reason I had before: to correct the past.

—Twyla Tharp, *choreographer*

Married, divorced! Married, divorced! But where Love leads I always follow.

—Clare Boothe, *playwright,* in *The Women*

Divorced, beheaded, died
Divorced, beheaded, survived.

—*Mnemonic for the fate of Henry VIII's wives*

When [Dad] heard that Will had been married before and had not made a go of it, he would consider him a bad risk, like a corporation which had once already been liquidated.

—Alison Lurie, *novelist,* in *Love and Friendship*

With Gary, I've become a woman with a capacity for happiness again.

—Lucille Ball, *comedian,* on her second marriage

The room was filled with people who hadn't talked to each other in years, including the bride and bridegroom.

—Dorothy Parker, *humorist,* about the second time she wed Alan Campbell

Live and unlearn. Dr. Johnson said that a second marriage is the triumph of hope over experience, to which I would add that the third is more like the triumph of compulsion over both.

—TED SOLOTAROFF, *editor*

I never had to wear an ugly bridesmaid dress—I've never been a bridesmaid . . . always a bride.

—VICKI L. WAYMAN, *realtor and upholsterer*

Like any other woman who has been married before, my idea was to have a perfectly simple dress and a perfectly simple hat to go with it.

—WALLIS SIMPSON, twice divorced, before her marriage to the former king of England

We've been in every kind of relationship—in and out of marriage—and none of them works.

—PAULA SCHER, *graphic designer*, on being the second and fourth wife of graphic designer Seymour Chwast

Joan Rivers asked, "Is it true that the towels in your house are marked 'His,' 'Hers' and 'Next'?" I replied, "Darling, I don't bother to have *anything* embroidered on them. Nobody's ever lasted that long."

—JOAN COLLINS, *actor and novelist,* after her fourth marriage

Five husbands, each for ten years, would be just about right.

—INGRID BERGMAN, *actor*

A. You look exactly like my third husband.
B. How many times have you been married?
A. Two.

—JUDY PRIGAL, *New York Magazine* Competition #893

What had Tom's three marriages meant? Did they represent a helpless reaching out for happiness, or an aptitude for error?

—CAROL SHIELDS, *novelist,* in *The Republic of Love*

I didn't have any failed marriages. I've been married three times and each marriage was successful.

—MARGARET MEAD, *anthropologist,* divorced three times

It's still more likely to be a man, not a woman, who marries two, three, or even four times. Apparently trophy grooms are harder to find.

—MAGGIE MAHAR, *journalist*

Making a mistake takes too much out of you.

—JACLYN SMITH, *actor,* vowing not to remarry, after her third divorce, before her fourth marriage

Whenever you want to marry someone, go have lunch with his ex-wife.

—SHELLEY WINTERS, *actor*

The philosophy of a divorced and happily remarried friend of mine: "Better one for two than zero for one."

—JOSEPH TELUSHKIN, *rabbi and writer*

After stepping up to bat five times, I finally hit a home run.

—HENRY FONDA, *actor,* on his fifth and final marriage

Henry is a very moral man. If he were not, he wouldn't have married so many times.

—SUSAN BLANCHARD, *second wife of actor Henry Fonda,* commenting on his fifth marriage

So I haven't married today. But give me time. It's only eleven o'clock in the morning.

—MICKEY ROONEY, *actor,* between the sixth and seventh of his eight marriages

Forget about passion. Marry a man who will fix your toilet on Sundays.

—ERMA BOMBECK, *humorist*

A premarital agreement can protect [children from a first marriage] and, by allaying their fears, protect your second marriage. If the kids aren't worried about losing out financially, they're more likely to accept a second spouse.

—GARY SKOLOFF, *matrimonial attorney*

It's not that marriage itself is bad; it's the people we marry who give it a bad name.

—TERRY MCMILLAN, *novelist,* in *Waiting to Exhale*

To show that you're entering the union with at least some hope of success, consider a [prenuptial] contract that expires at a certain point. And if you're still not comfortable with the idea of an equal partnership after, say, 10 or 20 years of wedded bliss, you might ask yourself: Why am I marrying at all?

—MAGGIE MAHAR, *journalist*

A remarriage usually involves at least three family trees and cultures, as well as a history of loss and a struggle for fulfillment.

—CLIFFORD J. SAGER, HOLLIS STEER BROWN, HELEN CROHN, TAMARA ENGEL, EVELYN RODSTEIN, and LIBBY WALKER, *therapists,* in *Treating the Remarried Family*

Anyhow, the difference between one man and another does not amount to much.

—Virginia Woolf, *novelist and essayist,* in *Mrs. Dalloway*

All things can be replaced except the wife of one's youth.

—Talmud, Sanhedrin 22a

The judge decided to give my husband sole custody of all three of his teenage kids [from his first marriage] . . . starting tomorrow. I responded the way any decent, unprepared woman with no domestic skills would—I sprinted inside the house and called my mother.

—Ann-Margret, *actor*

I'll give you the future if you'll forgive me my past.

—Kenny Rogers, *singer,* at the ceremony for his fifth marriage

"Life Is Beginning at Last"

Rebirth and Renewal

You feel like two people at once: an old woman who has lost everyone and a girl whose life is beginning at last.

—Jane Shapiro, *short story writer*

Better to be a free bird than a captive king.

—*Danish proverb*

I can only say that my divorce saved me. I weigh ten pounds more and feel hundreds of pounds lighter.

—Ann Hood, *novelist*

In spite of the fact that randomness seems to govern our lives, I still believe that life is like a movie and you have the power to write your own script. It may not be *Mary Poppins,* but it needn't be *The Bride of Frankenstein,* either. Mine, of course, is *Saint Joan.*

—Joan Rivers, *comedian*

A biography is considered complete if it merely accounts for six or seven selves, whereas a person may well house as many as one thousand.

—Virginia Woolf, *novelist and essayist*

You have everything you need inside of you right now to live the life you are dreaming of.

—Barbara De Angelis, *relationship expert*

Divorce will never create happiness, but it can create an environment for future happiness.

—Raoul Lionel Felder, *divorce lawyer*

I bought a small picture of pink hearts. Its symbolism may or may not be romantic. Perhaps it is about life in general—a lightness, a joy, a giving that I want to cultivate, still believe in, despite the divorce.

—Tracy Salvage, *painter and teacher*

I have to believe that when the end comes it pays to cut your losses, there is almost always more ahead than we can guess.

—Mary Catherine Bateson, *anthropologist*

"The faults of married people continually spur up each of them, hour by hour, to do better and to meet and love upon a higher ground," Robert Louis Stevenson wrote. It was given to me to learn and grow in divorce.

—SUSAN SPANO, *travel writer*

You turn a corner and your whole life changes.

—*Yiddish proverb*

Divorce can be a great gift. The pain of divorce can be parallel to the pain of birth: it's scary, but you would not stop it. Nothing is wrong. Divorce can be like the birthing process. What may be emerging is the potential of someone more whole than before.

—JOSEPH JASTRAB, *psychotherapist*

Index